How Highly Successful People & Leaders Communicate

Harnessing the Power of Effective Communication and Influence. The Powerful Guide to Mastering Communication for Personal and Professional Success

by

KYE MONTGOMERY

ROAD TO SUCCESS

Table of Content

How to Access Your Bonus Content

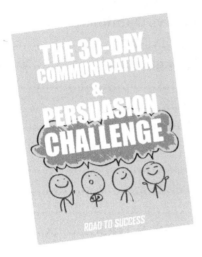

1) If you have not done it already, go to the end of the book, section "Get Your Bonus Content", and learn how to access. Accessing the Bonus Content first will benefit you in going through this book.

2) Let us know how thrilled are you about having this book by leaving a quick review (it will take 1-2 minutes) by scanning the QR code below. The best way to do it?

- Upload a brief video with you talking about how you feel about the book.

- If that is too much, not a problem at all! A review with a couple of pictures of the book and/or just with a sentence or two (although the longer the better!) would be very helpful!

P.S. You do not have to feel obliged but for independent publishers reviews are the lifeblood. It will be very appreciated, deeply valued, and it helps a lot independent publishers like us.

Scan the QR-code below to leave a review

| Part 1 | Understanding The Basis Of Communication

Section 1: Introduction

Have you ever wondered how people during the prehistoric times communicated with one another?

Prior to the invention of languages and words, humans were still able to interact at that time. Communication was achieved through a variety of means, including grunts and other sounds, signals and hand gestures, physical signs and symbols, and bodily movements such as dancing and acting. These methods allowed people to socialize and express their thoughts and emotions.

Cave paintings were another common means of communication during that era. There are plenty of these that have been discovered over time. And up to this day, some of them are still being uncovered in various parts of the world. These paintings depicted a wide range of subjects, including hunting scenes and religious practices. They are believed to have been used to transmit knowledge from one generation to another, convey information, engage in social communication, and support spiritual purposes, among other things. As such, they played a significant role in communication in those times.

Communication has always been vital to human existence, dating back to the beginning of our species. It has been essential for a peaceful and meaningful life, as well as for the growth and development of civilizations. Today, it continues to serve the same purpose of socialization and connection, plus a whole lot more. It's at the heart of human interaction and is crucial in building and maintaining personal relationships, learning and teaching, preserving and passing on information, producing entertainment and art, doing business, and raising awareness for social change.

What is Communication?

Communication is the process of exchanging information, ideas, thoughts, and feelings between two or more people through various means of expression. It also involves understanding and sharing meaning, just as indicated in its Latin root word *communicare* — meaning *to share* or *to make common*.

There are four important keywords or concepts that we have to give attention to in order to fully grasp the meaning of communication. Here they are:

Process

It's important to note that by *process*, we refer to a dynamic activity that continuously changes. In an ordinary conversation between you and a friend, for instance, a lot of changing thoughts and feelings may occur. Each of you reacts and responds to the message received, then comes up with another message to keep the conversation going. Hence, communication also involves cause and effect. It's an ever-changing activity from which varying outcomes are produced.

In this process of communication, there are three elements involved — the sender, the message, and the receiver. The sender encodes a message and transmits it through a medium or channel, such as speech, writing, or non-verbal cues. Afterwards, the receiver decodes the message and responds to it, which completes the communication process. This will be discussed further in another chapter.

Have you played the game called *Pass the Message*, also known to others as *Telephone*? In this game, each team forms a line. The first one receives a message which has to be passed on to the person behind him and so on until it reaches the last one in the line. Usually, the last person conveys a different message already by the time it gets to them.

This game is the perfect example of how communication works and why it's very important. Here we can see the *process* at work, with each group or each line being given the same message but getting different results at the end. In addition, at every stage of passing the message down the line, there are changes happening but the process keeps going because of the continuous contribution and interaction.

Understanding

Another important concept in communication is *understanding*. People can have different perceptions and interpretations of the same message. Therefore, the communication is deemed effective when the message is transmitted accurately and understood correctly. In this regard, other factors come into play such as the sender's tone, language, context, and even cultural background.

In the game described above, participants usually don't have the time to ensure that the message was received and understood well. Because of the time pressure and factors like people's ability to memorize, the message often gets changed. In such case, effective speaking and communication were not applied.

Sharing

Imagine yourself writing a reflection in your journal about your day, or doing a video call with a loved one who lives far away. Picture yourself attending a seminar online or going to a face-to-face live concert. These situations are examples of *sharing*, which is another principal concept in communication.

Sharing in communication can involve just one person (referred to as intrapersonal communication), two persons, or a group (three or more persons).

Going back to our game example, the process presumably involves a group of people lined up to pass the message from the front to the back. Here we are able to witness a joint activity in which a particular message or piece of information is shared.

In any form of communication, *sharing* must be present.

Meaning

Try looking up the word "bank" in the dictionary or even on Google. You'll see that this word has several different meanings. It can refer to a financial institution where we go to save our money. It can also mean a sloping land, such as a river bank. This word can also be used to mean tilting, such as when a motorcycle is banking on the road. There are other meanings aside from this.

If one word can mean a lot of things, then a whole message can certainly have various meanings too. This is why plenty of people experience misinterpretations and misunderstandings.

Meaning is very important too because it is what's shared in communication. The receiver must look at the context clues and ask questions to capture the correct meaning that the sender wants to convey.

Section 2: The Purpose of Communication and Speaking

If you've ever watched a ball game wherein everyone in the audience is mute and deaf, the whole place would probably be silent but you'll see them all jumping up and down from their seats and doing their visual form of clapping — raising both hands in the air and shaking them rapidly while smiling widely. This is their way of communicating their applause and cheer as well as expressing excitement and enthusiasm.

The mute and deaf also make use of sign language to "speak" to each other, to communicate personally or even in delivering a speech. This goes to show that people are made to communicate and will find ways to do so because it serves many important purposes in life.

Communication is of utmost importance in our daily lives, as it serves as a gateway to connect with others. It is a great way for people to exchange thoughts, feelings, and ideas, which is an essential part of daily living. When we communicate, it helps with building and sustaining relationships. Just imagine if you stop talking to your spouse or kids for years! Or you ignore the people in your household most of the time. What do you think will happen? This goes to prove our point — that communication is key to human connection and relationships. What's more, we should remember that it also empowers us to accomplish our objectives. Sometimes, the words that come out of our mouth or that we communicate through other means can have such a huge impact that it inspires others to take action. Other times, our messages simply entertain or provide joy and enlightenment, but this is not to be taken lightly. Who knows? Perhaps a piece of your writing or spoken advice, or a story you shared, cheered up someone who was on the verge of depression.

A common way that people communicate is through speaking. Every single day, we get to converse with a variety of people — some of them individuals that we regularly interact with, while others are those we encounter for the first time. Speaking is certainly a key tool for getting your message across, whether you're just chatting with your buddies or attending a work meeting.

There are other ways to express ourselves, though, such as by using body language or through writing. These days, there are also several ways to utilize the Internet for communication, like when we place a comment on social media or we use a chat platform or even email. Each mode of communication has its own pros and cons. We have to remember that different situations may require different approaches. There are more effective means of communication, depending on what the situation or purpose is.

Regardless of these modes, the ultimate goal is to learn how to communicate effectively. This is indispensable because it can do wonders for so many aspects of our lives — career, business, relationships, health, leisure, spirituality, personal growth.

Take a look at these seven main purposes for communication and speaking:

Sharing Knowledge or Information

Sharing knowledge or information can be very powerful. Just imagine the limitless ways it has become so useful in your life and in others' lives! Perhaps there was a time when you provided directions to someone lost on the road and this allowed him to reach his destination and avoid getting hit by a hurricane. Maybe you've experienced giving tips to a new employee on what she should do for the job. Or in the past, you could have received vital information about avoiding fire hazards at home. All of these examples show that sharing info to people is important in daily living.

In this modern day and age, we encounter a lot of people on social media who give tips and knowledge about something they learned about or experienced before. At times, a stranger might come up to us to ask for directions. Then we describe it with words. That's speaking! That's communication with the purpose of sharing information.

Take note that when we provide facts or talk about a certain topic, when we give instructions on how to do something particular, or when we share our skills and knowledge to an audience, we are giving out information that will give them something new to learn or apply. It helps others understand or improve something or maybe take action through a specific task.

One specific real-life example is the case of Edward Snowden, a former National Security Agency (NSA) contractor who leaked classified information about the US government's surveillance programs in 2013. His disclosure revealed that the US government was conducting mass surveillance on its citizens, collecting phone records, internet data, and other personal information without their knowledge or consent. This revelation sparked a global debate on privacy, security, and the role of governments in surveillance, leading to significant reforms in US laws and policies related to intelligence gathering. It also led to changes in the way governments and technology companies approach data privacy and security. What's more, the public became more aware of the risks and benefits of modern communication technologies. Although Snowden's actions were controversial and he'd faced legal consequences, his decision to share information had a profound impact on global conversations around privacy, security, and freedom of information.

Expressing Thoughts and Emotions

Chances are, you've already confided in someone you're tight with at some point in your life. We're all human, and sometimes we just need to get some stuff off our chest. Maybe you wanted to share your latest bright idea, vent about a tough situation, or just tell someone how you're feeling. It's human nature. We all need a confidant at particular points in our lives.

Human beings have this need to share thoughts and feelings with others. So yes, this might appear simple and natural, but it's a big purpose for communication.

Think of what kind of life you'd have if you were living by yourself in the mountains with no one to talk to. Maybe you'll end up communicating by drawing on the cave walls or creating some art work from natural materials in order to express your ideas and emotions. See? Even in such a situation, people are bound to want to share what's inside of them.

When we're feeling good, it's natural to want to shout it from the rooftops. And when times are difficult, it can be cathartic to talk it out and get some support. How about when we're really fired up about something? We might even put pen to paper or hit record on a video rant. It's all about expressing ourselves and connecting with others. That's just how we're made.

When humans open up to others, we're building stronger bonds and understanding each other better. It's all part of being human and finding our place in this world.

Building and Maintaining Relationships

Relationships are important to people. This is why we have counselors, therapists, mediators, and the like who address concerns and problems in marriages, friendships, teams, etc. These professionals always indicate communication as one of the keys in having healthy relationships.

Communication allows individuals to connect and form bonds, some of which can really last a lifetime. It's essential in a relationship because it's your means to express what you're going through, what you're feeling, what your expectations are, and what your needs are. These are all crucial in building and maintaining a relationship.

Speaking, in particular, can be full of impact. We have to be careful with our words because we might say something out of great emotion that could hurt someone. These words may be carried on for a very long time by the person who was immensely affected.

For instance, children who have been verbally abused may carry the effects up to their adult lives. Words from their past can influence how they think, speak, react, and act.

Another clear example is a couple arguing. One verbal fight could lead to a divorce! Imagine that.

On a positive note, though, children who grew up in households where family members often speak in an encouraging and loving manner frequently develop high self-worth and generally turn into happy people.

Persuading or Influencing People

One of the purposes of communication and speech that goes way back decades ago is persuasion. Leaders delivered speeches to sway people with regard to their political views or to influence the audience toward a particular religious ideology.

On a smaller scale, an ordinary individual has probably experienced having to explain why they want or deserve something. In the past, you might have asked a friend for a favor, gone through a job interview, or begged your parents to buy something for you. These are examples of persuading or influencing people.

At present, social media influencers got their label because they gained many followers who believed in them and who took actions and made decisions based on what they said. In such a scenario, we can see how communication and speaking are used for the purpose of persuading or influencing others.

Negotiating

Have you tried negotiating for a price on goods or services without using any words? That would have been a daunting task, unless both parties are using sign language and still understanding each other. Or have you ever negotiated with someone in another country who spoke a different language? It's certainly stressful and mind-blowing!

Communication is also applied in negotiation, most especially speaking. Perhaps you've tried negotiating with your parents about your curfew or with your teacher about your grades. Maybe you've negotiated with a supplier or client for your business. Or there could have been a time that you had to negotiate with your employer about your salary raise.

In all of these examples, the easiest, fastest, and most effective way to go about it is through speaking. Communication and speaking are essential for negotiation.

Providing Feedback

Imagine yourself going through life without receiving any feedback. For someone who never gets reprimanded or even praised, or who does not receive comments about their performance at home, in school, or at work, it might be difficult to become aware of your shortcomings and of what you're good at.

It's essential that as we go through life, we are conscious of our strengths and weaknesses. Knowing what we do best will enable us to pursue particular goals that can impact our lives.

Meanwhile, we can also work at what we're not so good at. This way, we'll always be motivated to be better.

Let's say you're an athlete. Aside from either winning or losing, you might not find out about your advantages and limitations if not for the feedback given by a coach. How about if you're new at your job? Isn't it vital to have a mentor who can inform you what you're doing correctly and which things you need to still work on? In the workplace, there's an evaluation system in place for the main purpose of giving feedback and helping employees improve. It's because this form of communication is valuable to us.

At home, when your parents tell you that you need to clean your room or work on improving your grades, these are also considered vital signals for you to change something. Such feedback can lead you to be a better person or even to develop a new skill or talent in the process. If no one bothered to communicate to you what you're doing wrong or what's lacking, you might just keep on doing it, not realizing that it's causing negative things in your life.

Communication is definitely useful for providing feedback. This can even come in different forms like a written evaluation, a spoken review or commentary, and even nonverbal reactions.

Feedback is highly fundamental because it can provide encouragement, help improve performance, build confidence, and develop new skills.

From the time we were babies, we'd already gotten feedback such as when parents tell us what we should or should not eat and touch. In school, we received feedback through grades, narrative reports, and conferences with teachers. At work, we are usually given reviews and evaluations. In business, clients are usually the ones who provide the feedback that can guide us on how to further improve and what must be changed in the future.

Such feedback are communicated to us through various channels and forms.

Entertaining

Did you know that entertainment had always been given value in communities? Storytelling in gatherings and theatrical performances have always been a popular form of entertainment, both of which make use of communication and speaking.

Music, another very old form of entertainment, came with chants and lyrics even during the Middle Ages. It was primarily religious in nature at first, but eventually grew into a vehicle for individual expression.

Today, we have a variety of actors, comedians, and speakers who entertain us through their speeches. And in a more personal context, we are able to entertain friends and even strangers by sharing real-life stories, telling jokes, and giving performances with words.

At this point, try to recall those times when you used communication and speaking for each of these purposes. Think also of the moments where you were the one at the receiving end.

In doing this short reflection, it helps us appreciate the importance of communication and speaking. It makes us more aware of how else we can utilize this to make our lives better.

Section 3: What is Effective Communication and Why Is It Important?

Have you ever attended an event wherein the emcee speaks softly or with uncertainty and doesn't have command of the audience? It's quite pitiful. Everybody in the audience ended up chatting with one another or not paying attention to what was happening on stage.

Have you ever met someone who's known as the "quiet type"? You know, the kind of person who hardly ever speaks up and just goes with the flow? Establishing a connection or building a solid relationship with that person can be a real challenge.

Or maybe you've been in a heated argument where neither side is willing to back down? It can be really tough and frustrating. No matter how long you argue, it can be hard to truly understand each other.

These examples show us how ineffective communication can really mess things up or prevent us from achieving some of our goals. That's why it's so important to do our best to improve our communication skills. We need to learn how to speak effectively and use other forms of communication to help us achieve our life goals, strengthen our relationships, and more. It might not seem like a big deal, but effective communication can actually make a huge difference in our overall happiness and fulfillment.

So, what exactly is effective communication? Basically, it's exchanging thoughts and ideas in a clear, concise manner. The message has to be conveyed in a way that the receiver can understand and interpret correctly. It also involves active listening.

In today's fast-paced digital age, effective communication is more crucial than ever. With so much information constantly bombarding us, we need to be able to comprehend and communicate effectively in order to succeed.

Indeed it's greatly important to learn effective communication for the following reasons:

Building Strong Relationships

Communication is the foundation of any strong relationship. It helps with building rapport and trust. Whether it's a romantic relationship, friendship, family tie, or professional partnership, practicing effective communication ensures that both parties understand each other's needs, feelings, and expectations.

Resolving Conflicts

Miscommunication can often lead to misunderstandings and conflicts. Through effective communication, the parties involved can be allowed to express their sides while also understanding one another's perspectives. Together they can work toward a mutually beneficial solution when they know how to listen attentively, use their words efficiently, and receive and understand the messages given.

Enhancing Leadership Skills

Effective communication is a critical leadership skill. Isn't it that we often choose leaders who are good at articulating their plans and ideas, painting their vision with words, motivating people, and providing clear direction?

Effective communication also involves listening actively and with empathy to the feedback and concerns of an organization or team.

Improving Workplace Productivity

Have you noticed in the workplace how things get done faster and more easily when people apply effective communication?

Effective communication promotes teamwork, collaboration, and a shared vision, which all lead to increased productivity and better decision-making.

Personal Growth and Development

Effective communication can also help individuals grow and develop personally. When we gain better communication skills, we can express ourselves better, understand others' perspectives, and build stronger relationships. It also enables us to reach out to more people for our personal, professional, or business purposes.

Creating Awareness, Shaping Opinions, and Inspiring Action

Public speeches and talks given by leaders have always been powerful tools for raising awareness and inspiring action. Why is it that until now, we can still watch particular speeches given by people from decades ago? Yet we continue to be moved. It's because they were so efficacious that they are still often shared and can still trigger certain thoughts, ideas, and behaviors.

Effective communication is truly remarkable because it gives us the ability to educate and influence people, as it has been proven throughout history. Today, in this digital age, we continue to see the increasing popularity of motivational speeches and inspirational talks.

Have you ever watched TED talks? These talks are known for being informative, entertaining, and inspiring. Delivered by innovators, leaders, and/or experts in various fields, they have also been shown to create great awareness while sparking inspiration and moving some people to action.

Moreover, if you've attended a seminar or listened to a leader who made you cry, laugh, or want to immediately act on what you just learned about, then you know that this is one person who effectively communicated their message. When a message is delivered compellingly, it has the power to motivate and inspire individuals to support a cause or become part of a movement.

Sometimes it can even be just a simple conversation wherein one person is sharing about their personal experience, and this story is contributing to the listener's general opinion or view about a certain topic.

Based on the examples mentioned above, we can gather that effective communication also has the ability to shape the opinions and attitudes of individuals about a particular topic. It can lead to behavioral changes that not only impact personal lives, but also have wider societal and even global implications.

That's why effective communication is so crucial, because it has the potential to initiate important conversations. Many times, people who are able to do this can raise awareness about vital issues and concerns, and encourage people to take action toward positive change.

Section 4: The Communication Framework Introduction

Imagine yourself watching TV or listening to the news on the radio. In this scenario, communication is one-way or linear because the person sending the message cannot see or hear instant feedback from the audience.

On the other hand, in normal human communication, such as speaking with one another or addressing a group of people, the process happens in real time. The sender can assess if the receiver understands the message, and the receiver can provide immediate feedback. This setup allows us to witness the communication framework in action.

So, what is the communication framework? It's a model that describes the process of communication, from the sender to the receiver, and includes the various elements involved in the process.

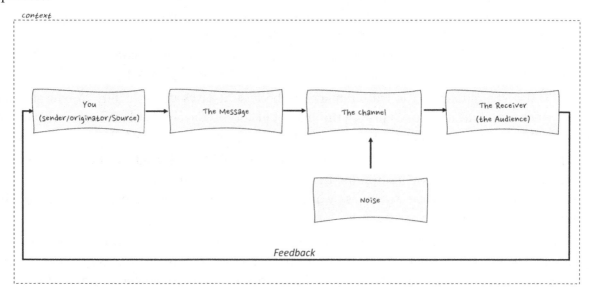

The Sender

The sender refers to the person who initiates the communication process and encodes the message to be sent to the receiver. This could be you who uses words and nonverbal signals like eye contact and body language to convey the message.

The Message

This is the information, idea, or concept that is given through speech or another channel. It may also include the emotions that you want the receiver to feel and understand. The message is not just composed of the words that come out of your mouth, but it also includes the nonverbal symbols you combine your language with. It also includes the tone of voice and style of delivery that you do.

The Encoding

The encoding refers to the process undertaken by the sender to convert thoughts and feelings and ideas into a format that can be transmitted through a communication channel.

The Delivery or Channel

This is the sensory route or medium where the message travels from the sender to the receiver. It can be face-to-face conversations, video calls, phone calls, emails, etc. Sensory routes refer to channels that make use of our different senses, but it's through sight and sound that most communication processes happen.

The Decoding

This is the opposite of encoding, which means that the communication received is transmitted back into thoughts by the receiver. It also refers to the process of interpreting the message and giving meaning to it.

The Receiver

The receiver refers to the audience or the person who receives the message of the sender and decodes it.

The Feedback

This is the response given by the receiver after interpreting the message from the sender. Feedback can be given instantaneously through speaking, right after the message is sent. It is the return message of the receiver to the sender. It can also be done via formal means such as through a letter or an evaluation form.

The Noise

In any kind of communication, there is a possibility of interference or disruption. The noise refers to anything that can interfere with the process of sending the message from the sender to the receiver. It also acts as a barrier that affects the quality of the message transmission and reception.

There are different types of noise — external, internal, and semantic. External noise refers to things that may interrupt the hearing, usually physical or environmental noise. For example, you're in a club with a live band playing loud music. Or perhaps a storm suddenly came and you can't be heard anymore. Meanwhile, internal noise comes from thoughts and feelings of the sender and the receiver. If a child is scared of his parent, it could get in the way of transmitting his message effectively. If you're listening in a seminar but you're worried about problems at home, those thoughts will interrupt the delivery of the message to you. Lastly, semantic noise refers to language barriers or the use of language that the receiver cannot comprehend. For instance, when you're in another country and trying to buy from a local vendor who doesn't speak your language, you will not understand each other. Another example is when an expert in a particular field uses jargon that the audience is not familiar with.

Now that we've gone through the components involved in the communication process, we have a better understanding of how they work with each other.

Can you see how the communication framework is a valuable tool? It makes us aware of each element at work. It provides us a guide on ensuring that the message smoothly passes from the sender to the receiver. What's more, it helps us realize what went wrong when the receiver reacts in a way we did not expect.

In essence, the communication framework is a roadmap that enables us to navigate through the communication process and achieve our desired outcomes.

| Part 2 | Becoming an Effective Leader & Communicator, Working on Yourself First (The Source, Sender, Originator)

Becoming an effective communicator requires first working on oneself. You must fully understand your own beliefs, values, and communication style in order to communicate authentically, confidently, and with clarity.

Barack Obama, former US President, is renowned as one of the world's greatest speakers and communicators. His speeches were powerful, inspiring, and persuasive because he demonstrated a deep understanding of himself. He was clear on his beliefs and values. He also consistently adapted his communication style to suit his audience. By incorporating personal stories and experiences into his speeches, he was able to connect with people from all walks of life while also building his credibility and trust with them. Obama delivered both formal speeches and informal conversations with equal ease, demonstrating his versatility as a communicator.

Even if you do not have to address a large crowd, it is still important to develop effective communication skills. Whether you are speaking to a colleague, client, family member, friend, neighbor, business partner, or anyone else in your daily life, your ability to communicate effectively is crucial to convey your message and achieve your goals.

In the earlier part of this book, we've already discussed the amazing benefits of effective communication. Now it's time to work on yourself as the first step in improving your communication skills.

Section 1: Identify Your Personal Values and Beliefs

When you're arguing with someone, do you find yourself never backing down and always wanting to win no matter what? Or are you the type of person who is peace-loving and willing to compromise instead of pushing to prove that you're right? During this argument or form of communication, what you value and believe in become apparent.

In an ordinary conversation, these values and beliefs often play a major role. For example, if you are discussing about education, some may believe that a traditional setup is necessary to discipline children. Others may want a more progressive, student-driven arrangement that allows kids to enjoy, grow more, and love learning. In such a discussion, a person's upbringing, culture, life experiences, background, and environment all contribute to what he values and believes in. These are reflected in his ideas and opinions, and his responses to the messages received from others.

What are Personal Values?

There's a saying that goes like this: "Values are like fingerprints. Nobody's are the same, but you leave them all over everything you do."

What you spend your time and money on, that reflects your values. Who you like to hang out with, that also shows what kind of people you value. When you make decisions, that's also a reflection of your personal values.

So what are personal values? Simply said, they're what we consider important in life. They shape our decisions and actions. We get them from our upbringing, environment, culture, experiences, and the people around us.

Everyone has their own set of values. The values we have may fall under the categories of security, achievement, conformity, self-direction, and more. These values guide us in making choices and can influence how we view the world. Some universal values that many people hold dear include respect, compassion, honesty, and responsibility.

Have you ever met someone who never cheats or would rather sacrifice their own interests rather than deceive others? Such a person values honesty, for sure. On the other hand, someone who values money and fame above all else might be willing to take immoral or illegal actions to achieve their goals.

What are Core Beliefs?

Core beliefs may be similar to personal values because people hold them dear and they also greatly influence our choices and how we deal with the world. They are fundamental beliefs that we possess about ourselves, the world, and the future.

For example, a child who grew up with loving parents may believe that they are worthy of love and attention and they are capable of forming healthy relationships. On the contrary, someone who went through physical abuse in their early years may believe that they're not good enough or that the world is not a safe place.

In some cultures, people may grow up to believe that they must always respect elders. Others may have the belief that they are responsible for carrying out the traditions to future generations.

Even religions can affect core beliefs. For instance, some religions may influence us to believe that we're sinful and inferior. Meanwhile, there are others that teach people to believe that they are inherently good.

Such beliefs are deeply ingrained in our psyche and can be resistant to change.

They are typically formed early in life and are influenced by culture, religion, upbringing, and personal experiences. They are also based on a person's direct personal experience with reality. They can also come from figures of authority in our lives, traditions we have in the family and in our society, and from our other associations.

There are two main types of beliefs — enabling beliefs and limiting beliefs.

The first one, enabling beliefs, refer to those that portray positivity, optimism, and self-efficacy. It's the belief that you're capable of something and that you can achieve something. Thoughts like "I am patient and hardworking" and "I always do my best and learn from mistakes" are examples of enabling beliefs.

The second one, limiting beliefs, refer to negative beliefs that hinder us from moving forward and keep us from achieving our goals. Because of these, a lot of people don't reach their potentials. Usually, these are inaccurate and damaging. They show judgments of ourselves and others that aren't true. Thoughts like "I am worthless" and "It's hard for me to make friends because people don't really like me" are examples of limiting beliefs.

A lot of common beliefs may have something to do with trust and self-worth. There are also those that deal with the nature of people and those that are about the future.

How Values and Beliefs Affect our Communication

Personal values and beliefs play a significant role in shaping how we communicate with others.

Our use of language, for one, shows these inner values and beliefs. A person who values equality will likely utilize inclusive language that ensure no one feels left out. He will certainly avoid words that may seem offensive or discriminatory.

Our nonverbal signals will surely also reflect what we value and believe in. For example, someone who values sincerity will look straight into the other person's eyes and may speak with gestures that indicate openness and genuineness.

Our personal values and core beliefs can definitely impact how we interpret messages. When we value open-mindedness, for example, we'll most likely make an effort to listen to others' opinions and perspectives. How about those who were put down by others when they were young? They may tend to jump to conclusions and get angry even when people at present don't mean something in a negative way. It's the mindset and the subconscious at work.

What's more, in resolving conflicts, it's very evident how values and beliefs also come into play. Have you met a person who grew up always having to fight for his rights? They may learn to believe in the importance of standing up for oneself. They probably place a high value on self-advocacy and assertiveness and may be inclined to speak up in a conflict and address the problem heads-on. Furthermore, when this person feels that they are being taken advantage of, they will tend to react at once and fight back.

How to Identify our Personal Values and Beliefs

Some of us may not be fully aware of our own personal values and core beliefs. In this case, it can be challenging to improve our communication skills. Want to become an effective communicator? Start by identifying these values and beliefs. It is an important step in self-awareness and personal growth, both of which are necessary in improving our communication skills.

In this case, it's important to take some time to reflect on our life experiences. Try to recall those moments when you felt fulfilled, happy, or proud of yourself. What values were you upholding then? What beliefs guided your decisions and actions?

At the same time, it's also good to think of the times when you felt bothered or uncomfortable. Did you feel violated during those times? What beliefs of yours were challenged?

Now this time, consider your role models. Who do you look up to, admire, and respect? What values do they embody and what beliefs do they have that you find inspiring or meaningful?

It's also helpful to examine your priorities in order to determine your values and beliefs. Which activities or goals are most important to you? Where do you spend most of your time and energy?

Spend some time reflecting on the questions above. Write down your answers to the questions and your insights as well, so you can have some clarity. In the process of writing them down and reviewing them, you will get to identify your personal values and beliefs. And when you are aware of them, you can manage them while communicating with others.

Section 2: Discover Your Purpose and Your Why

Do you sometimes wake up with eagerness or jump with excitement when an inspiring idea strikes? Do you also experience feeling weak and lazy, just letting each day pass you by without nothing significant happening?

If you said yes to the first question, then that means there are moments in your life when you clearly know your purpose for doing something, when you have a compelling "why" to drive you to action. But if you also said yes to the second question, it means there are times in your life when you feel like you're just going through life without meaning or purpose.

Each one of us has a unique purpose in life, but we need to find out what it is. We all have a reason for being, a compelling "why" that drives us. However, finding this purpose can be challenging. It's also not just a straight path, but can involve several twists and turns and detours. Imagine this — many people spend their entire lives searching for their purpose and never truly finding it. That may cause a sense of emptiness or a hollow and pointless existence.

It's important to take the time to reflect on your passions, strengths, and values to discover your purpose and understand your "why". Once you find the clarity around your purpose, then it can serve as a powerful motivator, giving you direction and helping you navigate life's challenges.

How to Discover Your Purpose

When we know our purpose, we tend to have that additional oomph to wake up in the morning, face the challenges of the day, work our asses off, and go the extra mile.

Reading is one way you can discover your purpose. It allows us to "travel" through space and time, to meet people who may be long gone, to understand various individuals, to learn of historical and cultural events that we are not exposed to in the physical realm. When we see the purpose of others in reading materials, we get to reflect on our own. We tend to see our own purpose too.

When we open ourselves to our own pain and the pain of others, it may also lead to discovering a purpose in life. For instance, someone abused as a child may be driven to start an anti-abuse campaign in the future. Someone who took care of a sick person may end up writing about the experience and inspiring others. A person who hears of another's painful divorce may suddenly be inspired to become a marriage counselor.

Apart from negative feelings that can lead to a sense of purpose, positive emotions can actually also do the same. We can cultivate behaviors and emotions that promote our well-being.

According to studies done by the Greater Good Science Center's Dacher Keltner, feelings of awe can open us to the realization that we are part of something bigger than the world we know, that we are connected to something larger than ourselves. Other researches about having a grateful mindset also show that people with a gratitude attitude tend to go out of their way to contribute to the world. In the same way, those who help others such as when joining outreach programs or volunteering at shelters are likely to lead a meaningful and purpose-driven life.

Another way you can discover your purpose in life is to listen to what others appreciate about you. For instance, a musician would often feel more motivated to create and share music when people praise them and show appreciation. A doctor will likely find purpose in saving lives when others thank them for doing so. Gratitude and appreciation can certainly direct us toward our strengths, which in turn give us clues on what our purpose is in life.

One more way that helps in discovering our purpose is through joining or building communities. People in religious groups or who belong to teams and organizations are likely to find their purpose more easily. Even your family, circle of friends, and colleagues at work are various groups that you belong to, and will likely also help you uncover your purpose. Because you have a common ground with the people in a particular community, it's likely to fortify your sense of purpose and even identity. For those who are having trouble finding their purpose, they can turn to the others in the community and try to evaluate what these people are here for and are fighting for. Check what impact they may have in the future, and see if this is the same thing you'd like to accomplish as well.

How to Find Out Your Why

If you're feeling stuck, uninspired, or bored with your life, then it may be because you are not yet fully aware of your "why". According to the German philosopher Frederick Nietzsche, "He who has a why can endure any how." Thus, when you've discovered your "why", it provides the strength, stamina, and perseverance to keep going even amid setbacks and difficulties.

In order to have goals that excite you and to enjoy your journey through life, you ought to find out your "why". This is your calling and conviction. This refers to the compelling reasons that drive you and push you to do the work you do and live the lifestyle you have.

Your "why" should come from within you and not from others. If you're in a job that resulted out of desperation or because your parents pressured you to take it, then chances are you're not enjoying it or you're not motivated much to do it. But if you're doing something because you believe in it and you're motivated to do it and sacrificing a lot for it, then that's something supported by your "why". It gives you meaning and purpose.

Self-awareness is important in finding out your "why". It may not happen overnight, but through constant reflections within yourself and about your life experiences. One way that you can develop self-awareness and eventually tune into your "why" is through journaling. If you write your thoughts, feelings, and actions on a daily basis, this can help you assess your desires and goals, and why you want these things.

Also start looking into your passions, strengths, motivations, and values. Your "why" could be hidden here. What gets you excited? What piques your interest and curiosity? What drives you to work and push harder? What makes you come alive? These are just some of the questions you can ask yourself to reflect on what your "why" could be.

It's also good to try new things. Why don't you explore new hobbies or engage in activities you've never tried before? You'll see how amazing it feels. And of course, what's important is how these can help you discover what you really enjoy and truly care about.

You can also seek feedback from others in order to help discover your "why". Just simply ask them to identify what they think your strengths are. Discreetly inquire what they think excites and motivates you. Sometimes there are things we are not able to see, but others can see about us.

Dig deep and ask yourself "why" multiple times. This is another effective strategy. For example, if your dream is to become a millionaire, ask yourself why. Perhaps it's because you want to provide for your family. But why? You may say that it's because you love them and want them to experience the good things in life. Then ask yourself again why. Maybe because you want them to be happy and you feel fulfilled when you see them enjoying a life of abundance. In this case, you might discover that your underlying motivation for building wealth is to make yourself and your loved ones feel happy and fulfilled. In doing this exercise, you can uncover the intrinsic motivations behind your behaviors and actions.

How Knowing Your Purpose and Your Why Can Help You

Studies show that people with a sense of purpose have goals that likely lead to launching important organizations, effecting change in the lives of people, and teaching things that can shape the world.

Having a purpose can make life seem more meaningful. For this reason alone, you'll feel more energized to start each day and to engage in your daily grind. Instead of getting bored or feeling unsatisfied, you'll love learning new things, meeting people, and accomplishing goals. You will also gain peace of mind.

According to a study published in the Journal of Positive Psychology, having a sense of purpose can be associated with greater happiness and life satisfaction. It can even be attributed to better physical outcomes.

Another study, this one published in the journal called Psychological Science, found that people with purpose were more resilient to stress and better able to cope with adversity. Wow, what an eye opener, right? This is why being fully aware of your purpose will surely help with mental, emotional and physical health.

In discovering your purpose and your "why", you'll find yourself moving forward with a clear direction and with greater motivation. You know what you want to achieve and why it matters to you. This can help you stay on track and overcome obstacles.

What's more, you'll see how it can lead to increased productivity and focus. You can get things done faster because you understand why you're doing it and what it is for.

In addition, having a sense of purpose and knowing your "why" will also lead to better decision-making. Easily evaluate options based on whether they support your goals and values. Make choices aligned with your purpose and "why". In the long run, you'll get to choose things in your life that are more satisfying and fulfilling.

Section 3: Discover Your Ikigai

Did you know that the Japanese people are known for their life longevity, having an average life span of 83.7 years? Over the past years, studies have shown that this statistic is closely related to the food they eat and to their health and wellness practices. However, in recent years, new studies have revealed that achieving life fulfillment through ikigai also contributes greatly to a longer life.

What is Ikigai?

Ikigai is a Japanese term that puts together the words *iki*, meaning "life", and *gai*, meaning "reason" or "value" or "worth". Hence, the literal meaning of Ikigai is "a reason for living" or "a sense of worth and purpose". It's an ancient philosophy that the Japanese have been practicing for centuries, and it is said to be the reason why they live long and happy lives.

Basically, Ikigai is all about finding the sweet spot between four important things: what you love, what you're good at, what the world needs, and what you can get paid for. In other words, it refers to your passion, your mission, your job, and your calling all rolled into one.

Come to think of it! These four things are the ones that can make us feel contented and gratified, like we're here on Earth for a bigger purpose and every day of our lives has meaning. What a great way to live life when you find your Ikigai! You'll definitely feel more fulfilled, purposeful, and balanced. Your actions and decisions in life can have a clearer direction that will make more sense.

How Can You Find Your Ikigai?

We all have our *Ikigai* deep within ourselves. It's only a matter of finding and unleashing it so that we can become fully aware of it and live life in alignment with it.

To find our *Ikigai*, it's important to ask ourselves four fundamental questions, pertaining to the elements mentioned earlier.

"What do I love?" This question refers to passion and may not always coincide with the other elements. Thus, you need to be able to turn your passion to profit and be able to serve others while at it.

"What am I good at?" This question refers to vocation. Your talents, skills, and abilities may not necessarily be aligned with your passion. You should therefore find a common ground and then connect it further with the other elements below.

"What can I be paid for?" This question refers to profession. A lot of people are unhappy with their jobs and therefore will need to find the intersection of this with the other elements in *Ikigai*.

"What does the world need?" This question refers to mission. *Ikigai* can only be completed when what you do involves service to the community or includes giving, which is more satisfactory than receiving.

What are the Five Pillars that Enhance Your Ikigai?

According to the neuroscientist Ken Mogi, also the author of the book *Awakening Your Ikigai*, there are five pillars that we can focus on to enhance our inner *Ikigai*. Here they are below:

Start small. When trying to awaken your *Ikigai*, you can start with small things, nothing too ambitious or fancy. This way, it's more effective and easier to accomplish. It makes us feel better when we succeed with small steps.

Accept yourself. This can be challenging for some people, but it's very important. You have to practice gratitude and self-compassion and not be too hard on yourself for your mistakes or weaknesses. Instead, forgive yourself and acknowledge your abilities. Move on from your disappointments and reward yourself for even the littlest achievements.

Connect with the world around you. It helps to immerse in nature or simply take a walk outside. Make time daily to turn off your electronics or put down your gadgets. Traveling also helps a lot! All these will help you learn more about yourself and the world around you.

Seek out small joys. When you learn to look for simple joys and little everyday things that can make you happy, you will feel happier, more grateful and more contented with your life. You can lessen the anxiety and other negative feelings within you.

Be in the here and now. Sometimes we tend to dwell too much on the past, or look too much to the future, that we forget to embrace the present moment. When we are in the here and now, we learn to listen better. Our energy levels increase as well as our motivation. We develop mindfulness and control over our thoughts and feelings.

Section 4: The Path to Fulfillment

At this point in your life, can you say that you feel fulfilled? Get to know yourself better by following a path to your own self-fulfillment.

Fulfillment is this internal feeling of being complete and whole, which is a state that should last for a long time, if not forever. It is achieved when we find value in how we personally impact other people and the world.

Fulfillment, according to psychologists, is also defined as the realization of our deepest desires and capabilities. It's an active process that a person must undergo.

According to a study led by psychologists Doris Baumann and Willibald Ruch from Switzerland, there are three things that are considered the components of life fulfillment — self-growth and pursuance of things that personally matter to you, living a meaningful and worthwhile life, and making a positive difference in the lives of others. Furthermore, some character strengths were also found to contribute to life fulfillment. Examples of these are hope, determination, and zest. In addition, traits like leadership and courage were also seen to have a huge impact on making people more fulfilled in life.

Based on research, there are three major universal motivations for people which lead to fulfillment upon the attainment of these needs.

The First Universal Motivation is Autonomy

Have you ever experienced feeling bad because you're obligated to accomplish a task but you don't really want to do it? This is the opposite of autonomy. For instance, a lot of employees around the world aren't really happy with their jobs but they continue to stay there because they feel that there's no other choice. Hence, in this case, they're not practicing autonomy.

Numerous individuals are motivated to liberate themselves from things that burden them, such as the need to constantly earn money for the usual expenses. Some risk plenty of things, even their own lives, just to fight for autonomy and freedom.

Autonomy is having the freedom to choose what you wish to do and avoid what you don't want to do. You make decisions based on your inner preferences and parameters.

However, not all the decisions we make based on autonomy are necessarily good for us. Sometimes, they make us feel great but may be harmful in the long run. We must be cautious. As we personally grow and develop, then this inner compass can improve too and serve as an excellent guide for choices based on the motivation of autonomy.

The Second Universal Motivation is Mastery

Try to think of the things you mastered when you were younger. Perhaps it was a game you played with your friends or a lesson you took up in school. Did it make you feel great?

How about recently? What were some of the things you got to master in your life? It could be in various areas of your life, such as knowing the inside out of your new job position in the office, learning a new sport or hobby, or conquering your fear of a serious relationship.

Oftentimes, we are driven to master something, which pushes us to work harder or persevere despite the odds. It creates that fire in your belly, which can lead to life fulfillment.

Try learning something new or finding ways to improve yourself in different aspects. Doing this will give you a greater drive for self-fulfillment.

The Third Universal Motivation is Community

Having that sense of belonging is essential to humans. This is why many of us enjoy taking part in various groups and organizations. We have clubs and teams in school, departments and committees at work, ministries and sharing groups in church, and so on.

In this digital age, you've probably also encountered or joined social media groups where people with the same interest gather together and discuss matters related to that interest.

Indeed community is one big motivation for people. Think of those you like to hang out with, contemplate on what you enjoy doing with others, and reflect on the benefits of being in a community. This way, you'll find out what to pursue and prioritize.

Being part of a community and getting active in such will surely boost your life excitement and fulfillment.

Section 5: Building a Strong Psychology and Mental Strength

Many individuals may traverse their entire lives without ever embarking on a journey of self-discovery. This lack of introspection can be a significant hindrance to effective communication, as expressing oneself and responding to others effectively require a deep understanding of one's own identity. It's challenging to communicate confidently and authentically when you're unsure of who you are.

Becoming a successful communicator involves developing a strong and positive psychological framework. Effective communication demands the ability to engage with people from all walks of life, empathize with them, and adapt to their unique perspectives. This requires a high level of emotional intelligence and what we refer to as mental toughness, including the ability to read situations accurately and respond with flexibility.

Furthermore, managing one's emotions is essential to successful communication, as unchecked emotions can quickly derail even a conversation with the best intentions. This requires a significant degree of mental strength, a trait that is shared among successful individuals worldwide. Without it, many of these individuals would have succumbed to depression or anxiety, which could have prevented them from moving forward in their lives.

Grit and Mental Strength

According to the study that well-known author, psychologist, and professor Angela Duckworth conducted, grit is the best measurement of high achievement. Her research tested Ivy League students as well as cadets at the elite US Military Academy West Point. The performance of these participants showed that grit counted more than intelligence, talent, physical fitness, and leadership ability.

Grit is the combination of passion and perseverance. It refers to the ability to maintain interest in and continue pushing toward long-term goals even amid challenges and setbacks.

Why is it that some people don't give up easily? Do you know of individuals who keep on pursuing their aspirations with energy and enthusiasm even when things become so difficult, even when they have to sacrifice so much? These people are said to have grit and are likely to become achievers.

The backbone of grit is mental strength, which is also the same as mental toughness. In order to develop this, here are some things you ought to remember:

You need to be able to withstand change and grow with it instead of shying away from it. Success coaches will always remind us that we will not attain personal growth and massive success within our comfort zone, but outside of it. The outside is referred to as the courage zone.

You must learn to embrace solitude and be comfortable in your own skin. Find time to reflect and spend a lot of "me" time. Accept and love yourself. This will enable you to know yourself better. It can lessen your stress and boost your mental well-being.

Focus on your strengths rather than your weaknesses. This will make you feel more positive even when you stumble along the way. When adversities hit, having a mindset that dwells on strengths can certainly make you feel braver and more confident about how you can resolve the concern and what you can do about it. Even your creativity and problem-solving skills will improve.

Keep going even after failing. There's a saying that goes. "Fail your way to success." Always learn from your mistakes and treat failures as lessons and opportunities to adjust and become better.

Let go of things from the past that do not serve you. This is done, so there's no need to dwell on it further. Just learn from the past and direct your energy to shaping a better present and future for yourself. You can then focus on what truly matters.

Approach life and success like a marathon. This means that you shouldn't expect your desired outcomes to appear immediately. Sometimes it might take time. Sometimes, you'll encounter problems first that will test you and your resilience and willingness to achieve your goals.

Always focus on what you can control. This is where you can start improving your situation if you feel like you've stumbled upon a major concern. Instead of complaining and blaming, just work on what you can manage. For example, if someone's spreading rumors about you, you may not be able to control that person but you can definitely control how you react. If your income dips because of economic problems in the country, rather than blaming the government or the country, perhaps it's a chance to review your expenses and savings, start some side hustles, learn better money management, and more.

Focus on your own journey and don't compare yourself with others. Remember that we are all unique with our own abilities and interests. Each of us is going through an independent journey toward success and happiness. When you keep comparing, it's like thinking that someone's achievements can impede yours. But that's not true because we live in an abundant world where we can all have a share of success.

Stop your pity party and stop playing the victim role. Sometimes, we may have a tendency to feel sorry for ourselves when things don't go our way. We assume that life is unfair, we're out of luck, or that others are more fortunate because of whatever reason. This is certainly going to bring you to the opposite of grit and mental strength.

Take action and don't let fear get to you. Sometimes, our minds tend to create various scenarios that make us fearful of things we haven't even tried or experienced. We should work on taking small steps toward our goals instead of fighting the fear or moving away from it. Just do it afraid, and you'll be surprised where it can take you.

Adversity Quotient

Have you heard of the term Adversity Quotient? What do you think it means?

If IQ or Intelligence Quotient measures a person's reasoning and cognitive ability, and EQ or Emotional Quotient measures one's ability to understand and manage emotions for dealing with situations and people, then AQ or Adversity Quotient measures the ability of a person to overcome challenges and remain resilient in the face of adversity.

When a crisis happens, you can immediately tell those with high adversity quotients apart from the ones with low scores in this intelligence. Those with good and excellent AQ will find ways to turn the obstacles into opportunities instead of complaining, blaming, and getting depressed.

Thus, someone with a high AQ is likely to also display mental strength and grit.

Section 6: The Importance of Having a Vision for Your Life

Try driving without knowing where to go, without a clear direction or plan. You'll probably end up aimlessly wandering around and wasting your fuel and effort in the process. After one whole day, you'll have accomplished nothing.

At times, we feel lost or unsure of where we wish to go. This is why we just go through the daily motions of life on autopilot. Maybe it's also why there are people who become so busy every single day but still unproductive and still without any significant achievement after many years. It's certainly easy to get caught up in the day-to-day grind. Then we lose sight of the bigger picture. That's where having a vision comes in.

A vision is a mental image of what you want to achieve or become in the future. It's the destination you plan to end up at when you're driving. It's your desired outcome that guides your decisions and actions. Without a vision, you may end up without direction or purpose.

A vision is not just about knowing where you're going. It also involves knowing yourself and being aware of the values and principles you have to guide you in getting there.

Take the story of Elon Musk, for example. In these modern times, he's not just an ordinary entrepreneur or business magnate. He's not simply a billionaire. He's considered a visionary man. Imagine this — he had a vision of revolutionizing the transportation industry through electric cars and space exploration! Some people mocked him and laughed at him, but this vision guided him to start Tesla and SpaceX, and to relentlessly pursue his goals despite numerous setbacks and challenges. It's definitely impressive and amazing! But the good news is that you can also be like him. Start with your own vision.

If your vision in life is blurry or hazy, you'll also end up making haphazard decisions or uncertain choices in life. You may end up wasting time and backtracking. Although it's fine to change your mind and direction, what's important is that you start working on discovering your purpose and molding your vision.

Why don't you take the time to reflect on your values, passions, and interests to gain a better understanding of what you want to achieve in life? This is a great way to get started! This process can involve setting goals and creating a roadmap to achieve them, as well as identifying any obstacles that may be preventing you from reaching your full potential.

Sometimes, it can also be helpful to seek guidance from a trusted friend, mentor, or professional. Additionally, taking time for self-care, such as getting enough sleep, eating well, and exercising regularly, can help clear your mind and provide you with the energy and focus needed to pursue your goals.

Remember, it's okay if your vision in life isn't crystal clear right away. Life is a journey, and it's normal to experience twists and turns along the way.

Why should you have a vision in life, anyway? Well, here are the top three reasons why:

Selection of Friends and Communities

Many people simply coast through life without any real sense of purpose or direction, content to live in the moment without much thought about the future. Do you anyone who's like this? If you're someone who's committed to personal growth and development, people who live like that can be draining and unsatisfying for you. You will no longer resonate with them. When you begin to notice that you're evolving in ways that differ from those around you, it's certainly challenging and at the same time eye-opening. This is the time when you may begin to look elsewhere for groups that fit into your vision, that help move you forward and provide more meaning in your life.

It's good to develop a compelling vision for your future, because you open yourself up to the possibility of attracting people and communities who share your values and goals. It's like a beacon that draws in individuals who are aligned with your mission and can help you achieve your dreams. For instance, suppose you aspire to become a highly successful sales agent. In that case, you may seek out marketing and sales groups. Wouldn't you rather spend time with such rather than hang out with friends who always just talk about music, fashion, and other people? You may also look to form close relationships with people who can add value to your journey, such as those who have achieved success in your field.

The good news is that when you have a clear vision for your life, it's much easier to attract individuals who share your passion or perhaps provide something beneficial in your path toward your making your vision a reality. Later on, as a result, you can build a supportive network of people who will help keep you on track and guide your focus as well.

Try it today! Close your eyes and picture that vision of yourself about ten years from now. Then try to see the path leading there. What would you have to go through? Who can be with you as you journey toward that vision? Now that those things have been clarified, then you know where to go and with whom to spend your time. It's a great way to foster a sense of belonging and purpose in life. It's also effective in feeling more motivated and inspired even when times get tough.

How We Make Use of Our Time

Are you aware that time is a finite and nonrenewable resource that many people often abuse? We tend to overlook this fact and therefore end up wasting plenty of hours on things that do not help us in any way. Sometimes we play mindless games or scroll through our social media newsfeeds for so long that we neglect our responsibilities and obligations. What's more, we might be throwing away days' worth of what could have been used to bring us closer to our dreams and goals.

But when you have a clear vision and it's immensely important to you to pursue it and make it a reality, then you'll notice how you're more careful of your time. You'll see how every minute begins to count and how you want to make the most of your hours to fulfill your purpose and bring you closer to your vision.

For instance, someone with a vision of becoming a doctor will likely spend their free time studying or volunteering at a hospital. Similarly, another person who visualizes becoming a writer in the future may spend their precious time reading books, attending writing workshops, and practicing their craft.

In your job, for example, do you feel that you're dedicated and driven to be promoted in one of the top positions? Or are you after making more money on your own and you're just using this job as a stepping stone toward a bigger goal? In such a situation, you'll surely see how your vision can affect the way you make use of your time and even how you deal with people.

Forming of Habits

Having a clear vision can be the key to forming habits that will help you achieve your goals! And all successful people will tell you that habits are crucial in building success and in achieving what you want in life.

When you have a clear vision, it's easier to develop daily habits and routines that align with your goals and values. For example, if you wish to be a healthy person, you might start a regular exercising routine, eat nutritious meals daily, and ensure that you get plenty of sleep. Now what if you're trying to become an effective communicator? In this case, you might find yourself practicing your speaking skills through regular conversations with different people or even through public speaking. Each day, you might take note of your progress and how the receivers of your messages and ideas respond. You'll probably also research tips on the Internet or pick up a book like this one that you're reading right now.

By developing such habits, you're setting yourself up for long-term success. This way, you can stay focused and driven. So, don't sleep on this! Take the time to define your vision and start building habits that will help you crush your goals!

In developing your vision, make sure that these elements are present:

The First Element: Purpose

Purpose is the reason for the existence of something or someone. It's the underlying motivation that drives a person to push forward with what he envisions. Hence, purpose provides direction and meaning to the vision. It acts as a guiding force to clarify your goals and objectives and thus propel you toward making your vision happen no matter what.

Remember that purpose is the rationale or the basis, while vision is the end goal — what you want to achieve. Without the first one, you will not be able to develop a clear vision.

For instance, if a person discovers that his life purpose is to help disadvantaged communities around the world, this could help mold a specific vision for him. One such vision could be to eventually put up a non-profit organization that provides health care and education services for children in such communities.

The Second Element: Picture

When we talk about vision, it usually enables us to picture the future. That picture is the mental image of your desired future state, and it's always been a powerful tool in inspiring and motivating people. This is why a lot of successful individuals teach others to do visualization techniques. When you can clearly visualize what you want, your energy and emotions change and align with it. Your inner world transforms, which allows you to come up with creative ideas in making that future a reality. It also provides added determination and grit amid setbacks.

The Third Element: Core Values

It's also important for your vision to incorporate core values. These are the fundamental beliefs, principles, or standards that guide your behaviors and decisions. It's the foundation upon which the vision is built. Naturally, you will only choose or develop a vision that's aligned with your core values.

Section 7: Understand Your Vision of the World

Do you believe that human beings are innately kind? Are you a believer of life after death? Do you always feel that there's a conspiracy involved when major occurrences impact the world, such as a global pandemic? Whether you answered yes or no to these questions, it's important to take some time to reflect and understand your beliefs about such things. There are many other questions that one may ask in order to clarify your vision of the world, of communities and societies, and of people in general. Such beliefs are also vital in shaping your understanding of yourself, and of your past, present, and future.

Your vision of the world is greatly influenced by your family, work, religion, culture, group of friends, and experiences. It is important to know that understanding this vision serves as the framework for how you see the world and your place in it. As a result, you can more easily identify your values, principles, and core beliefs. In addition, it allows you to understand your own motivations and desires and therefore be able to lead a more meaningful and purposeful life.

What are other things you may want to reflect on to fully understand your world vision? For instance, try reflecting on what you believe about wealth and material possessions because this might be influencing your money management and dreams in terms of finances. What do you believe about education? It could also be impacting your choices in life — which school to go to or where to enroll your kids, whether to engage in further learning in your adulthood, which goals to pursue. How about your belief on equality? It definitely influences how you interact with people, especially the ones who are close to you. Furthermore, what do you believe about governments? Are you one of those who constantly blame your government for your problems? This belief also shapes your actions. For instance, you may not be driven to find other sources of income if you're often dependent on the government. Or you may be driven to work for the government because you value it so much and know how it can greatly affect a nation.

Indeed these are various aspects that you have to look into in order to assess, accept, and appreciate your vision of the world.

Section 8: Continuous Learning of the World and of Yourself

No matter what you discovered about your own beliefs, values, and worldviews from the previous sections of this book, remember that they're not fixed yet. These can evolve or change as you move along life.

In developing better communication skills, we have said that it's important to get to know yourself first because you play a major and active role in the communication process. As the sender of a message or idea, everything that constitutes you will influence what comes out of your mind in words and nonverbal cues.

Have you ever heard of the term "Growth Mindset"? This concept refers to the belief that whatever we know right now is not fixed because we can keep on learning and improving our abilities through dedication, hard work, and perseverance. If we believe that we can always learn and grow, then our vision of the world will keep on evolving. What's more, we will keep evolving, and this process will continuously mold our principles, values, thoughts, ideas, and actions.

Lifelong learning is crucial to human beings because it can keep you relevant and make you more competent and confident. This is also a great way to spark new ideas and keep your life interesting. Your perspective can change, especially if your present one is not serving you.

So how can you keep learning about the world and yourself? Here are some ways:

Feel and accept your fears. Do you remember when you were in school and you had to be so conscious of your grades that the things you learned seemed to be meaningless but you just memorized them because they're necessary? Do you remember feeling scared and worried because your boss is going to evaluate your work? When these feelings are at play, it prevents you from truly learning. Hence, you ought to just feel and accept your fears as you learn new things and new skills. The next time you learn a new sport or hobby, don't worry about getting assessed or judged. Just have fun.

Keep a journal. This is a great way to never forget what you learn and to have a chance to look back on what you've learned in the past. You don't have to just stick to jotting down about your observations, activities, and feelings. You can record everything about the world and yourself, such as how new policies at work affect you or what your new habits are.

Explore and be curious. Being curious and having that desire to constantly explore come naturally for humans. Have you ever seen how a child is like? They're so curious about their surroundings that they don't give a care about failing or what others think. They are always observing and figuring things out. And when they make mistakes, they learn and try again. They move on. We must be child-like in this regard in order to keep educating ourselves.

Focus on the positive outcome. Have you ever received criticism or negative feedback? Instead of dwelling on feeling bad about it, you have to shift your focus to the positive that can come out of it. What's the payoff? Perhaps it's an eye opener for you to do things better and not be too complacent. Maybe it's going to make you a tougher person who's capable of more challenges.

Section 9: Develop a Growth Mindset

Why is it that there are people who seem to be willing to undertake challenging tasks that they are not familiar with while there are some who shy away from such, thinking that they will immediately fail? Why are there individuals who are not born talented and yet eventually become better than those with inborn talent?

The answer to these two questions lies in a person's mindset. A mindset is how you view yourself and the world. It's a collection of beliefs and attitudes that affect your way of thinking and also your behavior.

One type of mindset that has gained significant attention in recent years is what we call the "Growth Mindset". Developed by psychologist Carol Dweck, this mindset is based on the belief that one's abilities and qualities can be developed through dedication and hard work. It encourages us to embrace challenges and failures as opportunities for growth. It makes us see our abilities as malleable rather than fixed. Instead of thinking "I'm not born athletic", you can think "I'm not athletic right now, but with practice and training, I can be better at sports." Instead of saying "He's gifted that's why he's better than me", you can say "He's so good at it because he's been focusing, learning, and practicing. I can do the same too." Individuals with a growth mindset are more likely to take risks, persevere through obstacles, and ultimately achieve greater success.

On the opposite side of the spectrum is what's known as the "Fixed Mindset". In contrast, having this mindset makes you believe that all our traits and abilities are fixed. There are people who are born skilled and talented, and you can't really change your own. If you have a fixed mindset, you'll likely avoid challenges and you won't stretch yourself. It seems pointless to keep learning and training. When you encounter a setback, you'll likely either give up or blame others.

Consider a student who receives a poor grade on a test. A fixed mindset student may view this failure as evidence that they are not smart or capable of doing well in that subject. They may give up on trying to improve. Or it's likely for them to avoid taking similar courses in the future. On the other hand, a growth mindset student may view the poor grade as an opportunity to learn from mistakes and improve study habits. They may seek feedback from their teacher and peers, put in extra effort to understand the material, and take advantage of resources such as tutoring or online resources. This kind of student recognizes that their abilities can be developed with hard work and perseverance. They are willing to embrace challenges as opportunities for growth. As a result, the growth mindset student is more likely to improve their grades over time and achieve greater success.

What about a person who wants to learn how to cook a particular dish for a family gathering? Have you been in this situation, or do you know someone who fits this example? Reflect on how you or they went about it. A fixed mindset person may feel intimidated by the complexity of the recipe and doubt their ability to execute it perfectly. They may avoid trying and instead opt for a simpler dish or even order food from a restaurant. Meanwhile, a growth mindset person will likely view the recipe as a challenge. They will see it as an opportunity to learn new cooking skills. Heck, they'll probably enjoy the kitchen adventure too! In addition, such a person may research the recipe, practice it multiple times, and make adjustments based on feedback from others. The growth mindset person recognizes that cooking is a skill that can be developed with practice and determination. In the end, they're definitely more likely to develop some expertise in the kitchen while gaining confidence in their cooking abilities.

There's always room for improvement in developing a growth mindset. Besides, it doesn't work in extremes. Some people tend to have a fixed mindset in some aspects while they display a growth mindset in other areas of their lives.

Mindsets can definitely change, especially if you put in the constant effort. So how can you develop a growth mindset? Consider these ways:

Stop trying to get approval from others. This approval-seeking attitude can certainly trap you for life. You might just end up pursuing dreams and goals that make others happy but make you miserable. If you stop worrying about what others think, it will make you more comfortable dealing with your mistakes and failures. As a result, you can focus on learning and improving your own self.

Use the power of "yet" in describing what you know and don't know. Rather than saying "I'm not a good swimmer", you can say add the word "yet" at the end. See how it can instantly change your mindset and even how you feel about it. Try it now. Add "yet" at the end of statements that describe the things you don't know or that you're not good at.

Don't be harsh on yourself. Stop judging yourself and putting yourself down. Be mindful of your negative self-talk and replace it with positive and empowering language. When you fail at something, instead of beating yourself up about it, just focus on the efforts you put in. You tried your best and you're learning, so then there's bound to be a better result next time.

Embrace challenges. Let's say you've been invited to apply for a job promotion. This is both a challenge and an opportunity. Welcome it and work on it. Or if you're asked to lead a team for the first time, then don't shy away from it. Rather, learn more about how to do this well and give yourself time to improve and master the skills needed.

Take it one step at a time. There's a tendency for us to get overwhelmed and scared when we encounter challenges and difficulties. But if you divide it into small steps, you can take it on step by step. Gradual progress is better than quitting or not even trying.

Seek out new experiences. When you're always trying out new things, pursuing new interests, and learning new skills, chances are you'll cultivate a learning mentality. Why don't you take courses online or attend workshops? You'll also get to meet and interact with new people. Doing so will surely help you move closer to a growth mindset.

Remember that having a growth mindset is not similar to having a positive mindset. The former is all about working harder or smarter to improve and grow. The latter is about looking at the brighter side of things.

Section 10: Control What You Focus On

Have you ever noticed how easy it is to get distracted by things that don't really matter in the grand scheme of things? Whether it's the latest social media trend or the endless stream of notifications on your phone, it can be tough to stay focused on what truly matters. But did you know that controlling your focus is one of the most powerful tools you have for achieving your goals and living a fulfilling life? By consciously choosing what you pay attention to, you can become more productive, less stressed, and ultimately, more successful.

"What you focus on grows." This quotation is a simple, but meaningful way to remind us why it's important to control what we focus on. It tells us that the more we give attention and energy to something, the more it expands in our lives. With the many elements and stimulation we are frequently exposed to every single day, it can be easy to lose our focus or to shift our attention to things that do not serve us. Hence, we should be careful and always conscious. This concept is supported by research on the brain's plasticity, which suggests that our thoughts and experiences can shape the physical structure of our brains.

A particular study published in the journal called Neuron found that the brains of London taxi drivers who had undergone extensive training to memorize the city's streets showed structural changes in regions of the brain associated with spatial navigation. Here we see that the brain can adapt and change in response to the things we focus on and experience. Therefore, by intentionally directing our focus toward positive goals and outcomes, we may be able to shape our brains and ultimately create more positive experiences in our lives.

Focus on What You Can Control

In today's fast-paced and unpredictable world, it's easy to get overwhelmed by circumstances outside our control. It's natural to feel anxious and powerless at times. For instance, a change of management at your work may be beyond your control. Your teenage son's choices in life may also be out of your control. A natural calamity that strikes your city is another uncontrollable event. These things can definitely cause a lot of stress in people. Focusing solely on things we can't control can lead to frustration, distress, and a sense of helplessness. In contrast, placing more energy in what we can control can help us feel empowered and better equipped to navigate life's ups and downs.

Choosing to focus on what we can control is an important mindset shift that can have a significant impact on our well-being and success. By accepting the things we cannot change and directing our energy toward the things we can actually control, we can reduce our stress levels and boost our resilience. What's more, we can also increase our effectiveness in achieving our goals. For example, a mother who is anxious about her teenage son's college entrance exams may feel powerless to change the test questions or the grading criteria. However, they can focus on studying effectively, managing their anxiety, enrolling in review sessions, and finding out the acceptance criteria for the target schools. Similarly, a business owner may feel overwhelmed by a downturn in the economy, but they can focus instead on things they have control over — adapting their products or services, seeking new markets, and optimizing their expenses. By focusing on what we can control, we can take meaningful action, progress toward our goals, and feel more in charge of our lives.

Take the former First Lady of the United States, Michelle Obama, as a real-life example. In her book "Becoming," she shares how she coped with the stresses of public life by focusing on what she could control, such as maintaining a healthy lifestyle and prioritizing her family. And because she knows herself well, she decided to work on initiatives that were aligned with her values. She also described how she stayed focused on her goals and ignored criticism by learning to tune out the negative noise. Rather, she made sure to pay more attention to the positive impact she was making. It empowered her and drove her to do more, instead of dampening her spirits. Her ability to focus on what she could control helped her navigate challenges and achieve success in her various roles, including being a lawyer, a public servant, and an advocate for social change.

Focus on What You Have

When we say "control what you focus on", this includes focusing on your blessings rather than dwelling on problems and lack. You've probably met someone who never seems to be satisfied and who's always looking for what they don't have. This is a surefire way to make yourself miserable and stressed. But if you train yourself to focus on what you have, it will help you appreciate those things. It will help you develop what we call a "gratitude attitude".

Rather than constantly striving for more or comparing ourselves to others, taking time to appreciate the things we already have can help shift our perspective and increase feelings of happiness and fulfillment. Studies have demonstrated that practicing gratitude can bring many benefits for the body and mind health, including lower levels of stress and depression, improved sleep quality, and increased resilience. By focusing on what we have, we can also cultivate a sense of abundance and reduce feelings of scarcity or lack, leading to greater satisfaction and well-being in life.

What's more, it's important to note that focusing and building on what we have can lead to the development of new personal assets. When we are dealing with challenges, applying this kind of focus will surely help us identify practical, feasible options for the potential solutions.

Focus on What You Can Do

Focus really is a powerful tool that human beings are lucky to be capable of. Thus, we should make good use of this unique ability. Whenever we encounter a problem, we have to ask ourselves this crucial question — "What really counts and what can I do about it?"

Imagine this: You've been feeling tired and rundown lately because of a big project you're organizing and plenty of chores to do at home too. Because of this, you've neglected your health, putting off exercising and choosing to eat snacks on the go. This is the reason why your energy levels seem to be down lately and you sometimes feel like you just want to sleep and rest. In such a situation, ask yourself the question mentioned above. What really counts and what can I do about it? Through this question, you will get to evaluate what's more important to you. Is it your health and well-being? Or is it your project and house maintenance? Of course we can always strike a balance. You don't have to choose only one. But still, if you care about your body and you want to feel good and energetic, then you have to find ways on how to avoid your unhealthy tendencies even if you're busy. Let's say you cannot get out of that project, then perhaps you have other people in the house who are willing to take on some of the other chores. Or you can also stock up on healthier snacks that are easy to consume or bring with you. Another thing you can do to help you in this situation is to insert your exercise time into your other tasks. For example, choose the chores that will enable you to exercise, and walk or take the stairs when you're doing your project.

Shifting our focus to what we can do, instead of what we can't, can really change our mindset and open up new opportunities. By honing in on our strengths and abilities, we can build confidence and take action towards achieving our goals. It's kind of like a "can-do" attitude. Research actually supports this approach, showing that having a growth mindset - where we believe we can learn and improve, as discussed in a previous section - can have a big impact on our achievements. So rather than feeling stuck or limited by our current situation, focusing on what we can do empowers us to take control and make positive changes in our lives. Plus, it just feels good to take action and see progress.

Focus on What You Need

There are times when we are faced with so many options that we may lose focus or get distracted from our goals. It's important that you focus first on what you need before your wants.

What if you're at a party and there's a lot of food choices? If your current need is to lose weight, then you have to pay attention to that to guide you with what to eat. Another example is how you use your weekends. There are certainly plenty of options, but if you are presently in need of extra income, then maybe instead of going out with your friends, you can opt to work on side hustles or to turn your passion into profit.

Focusing on what you need can help you narrow down choices in life and make better decisions that align with your goals and values.

Furthermore, it allows us to zoom in on what's important because this is what is really needed. Sometimes, we tend to keep ourselves so busy with mundane things or with urgent matters that we forget to work on what we truly need.

Focus on What's Good

Focusing on what's good in your life or in a particular situation enables you to develop a positive mindset. It makes you feel great, boosts your energy, and increases your resilience in the process.

When we focus on what's good, we shift our attention away from the negative things that bring us down. Then we start to see the positive things that are happening around us. Let's say you're having a tough day at work. Maybe you're dealing with a difficult boss or a difficult colleague. Instead of dwelling on those negative aspects, try focusing on the good things that happened throughout the day. Maybe you had a great conversation with a coworker, or you received some positive feedback on a recent project. Try this now, and you'll surely love the long-term effects! By focusing on those good things, you can start to change your mindset and see the situation in a more positive light. It can also help us feel more grateful and appreciative of the things we have in our lives. So, take some time to think about the good things that are happening in your life, no matter how small they may seem.

Focus on Where You are Going, Not on Your Fear

If you've heard of the saying, "Keep your eyes on the prize," then you know how important it is to focus on the target or destination. This pushes you to keep going because your attention is on that prize instead of on the fears and doubts surrounding you and the situation on hand.

Imagine yourself playing archery. Your eyes must always be on the bullseye, not on the condition of your equipment, your competitors, or the audience. If you're nervous and frightened, that will simply lower your confidence and rattle you. But if you know that you've practiced hard and you visualize the end goal, which is where you're going, then that will motivate you to do your best and to concentrate.

Some say that F.E.A.R. stands for "False Evidence Appearing Real". This is true because when we are fearful, we make up all sorts of negative potential scenarios in our minds. We imagine the worst happening instead of the best. The outcome? You mess it up or you end up turning back and quitting.

Thus, always remember to focus on where you are going, not on your fear.

Balance Your Focus Between Past, Present, and Future

Some people focus on the past a lot, always beating themselves up for mistakes or dwelling on what could have been. There are also others who focus on the good things in the past, embracing the nostalgia, but that keeps them locked up in the past. They get to neglect working on new memories because they're too caught up in what was. They don't see the present clearly.

Meanwhile, there are also those who live for the present only. It's good to be in the here and now, but it can also be damaging if you don't use valuable lessons from the past to be better now and if you also don't care much for the future.

There are individuals too who are considered future-oriented, so much that they don't live in the moment when there's a significant event playing out. They overlook the experience and don't really absorb or enjoy it very much because they're already thinking of what they're going to do in the future. Or maybe, they do pay attention to the present occurrence but only in the aspect of how it will affect tomorrow. In addition, they also get to miss the past because that's just too far away and unimportant for them.

Each of these three is powerful. But there are disadvantages to focusing on just one. You have to balance all three to have the best results.

Because you are reading this now, you'll have the advantage of re-framing your perspective every time you find yourself veering too much toward the past, present, or future. Leaning toward only one or two can keep you from seeing the bigger picture.

Look at it this way. If you're trying to understand what a painting means, you cannot just zoom in or review the details without seeing the whole thing. You cannot just study the process the artist went through or simply look at the sketches that served as the artist's references. You must see everything and consolidate all the information. That will allow you to see the entirety of the picture or artwork.

Let's take this scenario for example: A woman dreams of getting married with her present boyfriend and having a happy family someday. She sometimes looks back on her past relationships and realizes that communication plays a significant role in strengthening the connection between a couple. She uses this lesson to make her current relationship much better. When she and her boyfriend exchange chat messages and write notes to each other, when they engage in casual or deep conversations, she is always attentive and responsive. She relishes the moment and makes him feel her presence. At the same time, she also plans for the future by discussing marriage with her significant other and by working with him to save up for their future life together. Now in this example, we see the past, present, and future working together for the best outcome.

We ought to balance our focus between the past, present, and future. Doing so will help us see the full picture, understand our situation better, and plan for a better and more meaningful life.

Section 11: Direct Your Focus with the Use of Empowering Questions

When you encounter a new experience or situation, isn't it that you tend to ask a lot of questions in your mind? Try to pay attention to the kind of questions that you have. Are they empowering or disempowering?

For instance, let's say you're going to climb a mountain for the first time. Here are some questions you might ask:

"Can I really do this?"

"Am I prepared for this?"

"What if I stumble and hurt myself?"

"Why am I overweight and unfit?"

"Why am I always getting left behind?"

These questions go with assumptions about yourself that tend to make you feel down and discouraged. People often ask themselves disempowering questions that lead to negative thoughts and feelings. This is why it's important to be aware of them so that you can consciously replace them with empowering ones.

Since we have thousands of thoughts passing through our minds every single day, we ought to use these to direct our focus to what will help us move forward, overcome challenges, and make it bigger and better in life.

Now let's try to transform the questions above into empowering ones. Read them again and see where your thoughts are going and what emotions are being evoked. These questions will enable a positive shift in you as you climb that mountain:

"How can I do this well and accomplish the goal?"

"What have I done to prepare for this and how can I use it here?"

"What drives me to do my very best?"

"What healthy habits can I form at this time to make myself fit?"

"How is this experience helping me to learn and grow?"

With these questions, you direct your mind to focus on the good things that can come out of the experience. You also get to give more attention to potential solutions rather than dwelling on the negative aspects.

Here are some other empowering questions for you to use:

"What's amazing and exciting about this situation?"

"How can this help me and others?"

"What do I appreciate most about myself?"

"What steps can I take to move closer to my goals?"

"How can I turn this challenge into an opportunity for growth?"

"What can I learn from past mistakes that will help me improve today?"

"How can I cultivate self-love in my thoughts and actions?"

"Who inspires me and why?"

"How am I able to inspire other people?"

"What is the bigger purpose behind my decisions?"

"What are my greatest strengths?"

"What do people ask me to help them with?"

"What do I love the most about this situation?"

"How can this person or situation help me become a better version of myself?"

"What can I learn or master today?"

"What drives me to push myself to the limits?"

"What triggers my passion?"

"What self-limiting belief has been stopping me from moving forward?"

"How can I turn this limiting belief into something positive?"

"What challenge can I turn into an opportunity for growth and how?"

"What would I do if I knew I couldn't fail?"

"Who are the people giving me strength and inspiring me?"

"How can I use my skills and talents to make a positive impact?"

"What self-talk do I use that holds me back from achieving my true potential?"

"How can I turn negative self-talk into positive ones?"

"What can I do to take better care of my mental, emotional, and physical wellness?"

"What things am I grateful for today?"

"How can I express more gratitude and appreciation in my life?"

"How can I create more balance and harmony in my life?"

"How can I build deeper and more meaningful relationships in my life?"

"What legacy do I wish to leave behind?"

"What projects ignite my passion and give me reason to keep going?"

"What are some creative solutions to this problem that I'm facing?"

"How can I enhance my personal and professional growth?"

"What would I do differently today based on lessons from the past?"

"How can I step outside of my comfort zone and learn new things?"

"What are the patterns or habits that are no longer serving me?"

"How can I break free from these negative patterns or habits?"

"What things bring me joy and fulfillment?"

"How do I apply and develop greater resilience in the face of adversity?"

"What wisdom will I share to others who are younger than I am?"

"What stories from my life empower others?"

"What skills or talents of mine have I not been utilizing?"

"How can I further develop these skills or talents that I'm not utilizing?"

"What are the bigger issues or causes that I'm passionate about?"

"How can I make a difference in the areas I care about?"

"What should I focus on right now?"

"What routines of successful people can I adopt for my own growth?"

"How can I let go of the past so I can move forward?"

"What boundaries should I set for my own well-being?"

"How can I make my work more meaningful and purposeful?"

These questions will do wonders for redirecting your thoughts, feelings, and actions toward the positive. Go over all of them many times. Read and understand each one well, so that they can be ingrained in your mind. From time to time, especially when you're feeling low or facing adversity, you can check these questions and ask yourself some. You'll realize just how powerful they are, guiding you toward a path of illumination that will allow you to focus on what's important and on what can be good for you.

Retraining Your Brain

Brain scientists and mind experts tell us that the brain is molded in our younger days, often during the first seven years of our lives. During this time, many of us frequently heard negative things from the people around us. Parents usually said "No!" when we tried to explore the environment. Also, you probably often heard your teachers say "Don't do that!" when we attempted to experiment with something we wanted to learn more about, but it disrupted the class. These small things have added up to make our brains lean on the negative most of the time. They have become instilled in our subconscious.

But don't worry! It's not yet too late. We can retrain our brains. It's very possible, and it has been done so many times before by various individuals and groups. First, we have to learn to be aware of our thought patterns. Are you always cynical or doubtful? What things trigger your negative thoughts? Are you often overwhelmed by your fears? Next, we have to scan for the positive things in these negative situations and elements. Check for the silver lining and focus on that.

In each situation, there's always the brighter side. If we look for it, we'll find it. But if we look for the negative, we'll also find it. But which one is going to help you improve your life in general?

Retraining our brains is not simple. It takes time and consistency, so you must work on it daily. For instance, every morning upon waking up, you can assess yourself and your life and use empowering questions to direct your thoughts, words, feelings, and actions. Instead of saying "Why the hell did I wake up late again?", you can try "How can I wake up earlier tomorrow?" Try asking each question to yourself and see how each one affects you differently.

Before going to bed, you can also do the same thing. Remember the things that happened during the day. Instead of asking "Why couldn't I finish that task at work today?", you can use the question "How can I complete that task tomorrow and what can I do to make sure I finish my future tasks on time?"

Questions can make all the difference in what we focus on. And what we focus on can certainly change our lives.

Shaping Your Reality and Future

One example of how what you focus on shapes your reality is the phenomenon of confirmation bias. Confirmation bias is the tendency to understand new info so that that confirms one's preexisting beliefs and values. For instance, imagine someone who believes that all politicians are corrupt and dishonest. Isn't it that they will likely assume this when they encounter any piece of information about politicians? If they hear about the mayor's new project, they'll say he's doing it to make more money because he's overpricing everything.

The perception of reality is shaped by our preexisting belief, and we may therefore overlook evidences that challenge our perspective. Conversely, someone who believes in the potential for positive change in politics may focus on stories of political reform or leaders who are making a positive impact. This person will also interpret the mayor's new project differently, perhaps seeing it as a sign of development in the city brought about by great politicians.

This shows that what we choose to focus on can influence our perception of reality, and the more we focus on a certain perspective, the more that perspective becomes our reality. By becoming aware of our biases and intentionally choosing to focus on different aspects of our experiences, we can shift our perception and potentially create a new reality for ourselves.

The bottom line is for us to ask more empowering questions to open ourselves up to many possibilities and alternative solutions to our concerns. It allows us to see a more positive reality and future.

Why Empowering Questions Help in Effective Communication

A lot of misunderstandings are rooted in people's differences in opinions and perspectives. Sometimes, a person misinterprets a particular piece of information because his reality and biases gave him a different type of meaning in contrast to what the sender really meant.

A simple joke in the workplace may be fun and harmless for the sender, but it could be offensive for the receiver and can even get the sender in trouble. Furthermore, you may have the tendency to always put people down when you're giving your opinion because you simply don't know how to pay attention to the brighter side of things. Perhaps for you, it's just a form of honesty. But for the other person, it's insulting and disrespectful.

Remember that empowering questions can shape our reality, just as much as disempowering questions can do the same in an adverse way. Which do you think will serve you better when communicating with others? Which do you think will people like and trust more?

Indeed we need to keep in mind that empowering questions that help us focus on solutions and opportunities rather than problems will make us understand and therefore express ourselves better. That's a sign of being an effective communicator. For instance, if you ask yourself the question, "What do I like about myself?" it can remind you of what's great about you and will influence how you communicate in a job interview or when you're in a relationship. This simple question can make a big impact already!

What's more, in being an excellent communicator, you must also be good in listening and understanding others. Now when you ask the empowering question, "How can I help others?" then it could help you truly focus on what they're trying to convey.

Remember that this kind of questions will also help in building trust and respect because ultimately, you'll demonstrate a genuine interest in the other person's thoughts and feelings. And when you have that willingness to support their growth, then it molds your replies and messages differently.

Empowering questions can also promote creativity, innovation and problem solving. When you have these hovering in your thoughts, you'll most likely consider new perspectives and possibilities. You'll become more open-minded. You'll get to foster a more constructive dialogue where there is mutual understanding and growth.

When you often ask empowering questions to yourself, your mind will always lean toward positive things. This, in turn, leads to empowering thoughts, words, and feelings. All of these will be reflected in how you communicate with others.

Section 12: Learn to Use Empowering Words

Now that you've learned all about empowering questions, it's time to learn about the impact of empowering words. Using such can definitely strengthen your focus on the positive and direct you toward something better.

There are particular words that we attach to experiences which can have either a negative or a positive effect on us. For example, when you look at your debts, you may tend to say "This is hopeless!" or "It's so depressing!" But what if you use the words "This is a sign for me to improve how I manage my money" or "I'm on the road to better finances"? The latter options will probably have a greater impact at pushing you to analyze your financial situation and giving you more ideas on how to get out of debt and avoid it in the future.

In shaping our destiny, we must always be conscious about the words we use or attach to particular people and experiences.

Change Your Habitual Vocabulary

If you are used to words that connote negativity and mediocrity, it's about time to transform them into empowering ones.

Perhaps you grew up in a household with people who are always in the complaining and blaming mode. Or maybe you grew up hearing individuals around you saying disempowering words. Most likely, you will absorb those words and utilize them in your own life. What if it has become habitual for you to say "I can't afford it" or "It's his fault"? It seems like in such cases, you're left with no choice and there's nothing you can do. It's like putting a barrier on the street that you can never pass through. But then, if you say "My money is coming" or "I am to blame for it", then you are providing yourself hope and thus pressuring the brain to come up with solutions and ideas. And because you're taking the blame, it means you are making yourself accountable. The good thing with this is that you realize you can change things because you're the one to blame for it.

Your vocabulary tends to assign the meaning to something. This elicits specific emotions as a result of the assigned meaning. Thus, a problem can affect different people in different ways depending on the words they use to describe or refer to it, which is the basis for the meaning. In our example above, saying "I can't afford it" can make us feel hopeless and inferior. Meanwhile, saying "My money is coming" can ignite hope and creativity and make you feel excited.

Aside from negative meanings and emotions, the use of mediocre vocabulary may also be disheartening or limiting. If you describe your efforts as just "okay" instead of "fantastic" even if you know you've been doing your best, that will not trigger positive emotions. If, after a powerful sales rally, your reaction is "It's good and I feel motivated", it may not have that much energy in it to propel you to action. But if your words are "It's totally incredible and amazing! I'm driven and passionate!", now that's going to push you to work harder to achieve your sales target.

So how can we transform our vocabulary? The first step is to commit to feeling good and developing a better life. This way, recognizing that disempowering words can bring about negative feelings and slow you down in attaining your dreams will make you more conscious in replacing them. You'll be encouraged to practice the use of empowering words if you truly want an amazing life for yourself. Afterwards, the second step is to associate more positive words with common things, people, and experiences that you used to attach negative words to. This kind of conditioning can definitely make you feel marvelous! It can bring you closer to the better version of yourself.

Replace Limiting Words with Possibilities

Do you have the pattern of "can't" hammered into your brain? If so, you've probably gone through moments in your life when you had an idea or wanted to try something new but you held back and ended up not doing anything at all.

This is just one example of a limiting thought pattern that we have to work on changing. Words like "can't" and "don't" and "not" may bring about a sense of self-defeat and despair. Saying "I don't know how to court a girl" or "I'm not talented like him" can be quite depressing. It's like you're already throwing in the towel and not even trying alternative ways. You're not even attempting to overcome this obstacle to get to your goal or enjoy life more. Imagine this — what if you just say "I'm going to learn and try courting this girl"? Or you say "I may not be talented like him in that arena yet, but I can definitely work on it and train myself to be highly skilled in it." Notice the difference in the emotions it's triggering within you when you use empowering words instead?

Many people grow old not even realizing that they're using limiting words all their lives. So you must give yourself a pat on the back if you're reading this, because you're one of the lucky ones to become aware of it. As a result, you'll get the opportunity to transform your limiting words into possibilities.

Remember that you can reclaim control and responsibility in your life, and therefore have the power to achieve your aspirations, if you focus on possibilities instead of limitations. Focus also on opportunities rather than threats. Sooner or later, you'll find yourself more blessed. You didn't just transform your vocabulary, but you transformed your life in the process.

Start today. Here are the steps you must take in order to replace your disempowering words with empowering ones:

The first step is to list down the limiting and disempowering words that come out of your mouth, or the ones that you commonly use. Examples of these may be "I really can't do it", "I'm not good enough", and "It's impossible".

The second step is to think of how these words make you feel. How do they affect you? What feelings are incited when you say these words? You must recognize that disempowering words can create not just self-doubt and fear, but also resistance to go forward or move on. Such words can bring you to low vibration energy, which can be felt by people around you.

The third step is to select the empowering words that can replace the disempowering ones you wrote down. For example, you can now start saying "I can do it", "I am capable", and "I will find a way".

The fourth step is to ingrain these new empowering phrases within you by practicing and using them daily. When you talk to others or even when you're just speaking to yourself silently, it's important to keep using them until you get used to them and the old, disempowering ones are completely replaced. Keep repeating the empowering words especially when you face stressful situations. This way, you'll reinforce positive beliefs and attitudes, and encourage yourself to look at the brighter side and focus on what you can do.

The fifth step is to also reflect on how the empowering words affect you and your thoughts, feelings, and words. Notice how they make you feel more confident, less stressed, more inspired and motivated.

The sixth and last step is to celebrate your progress and the small successes along the way. Don't be too hard on yourself when you slip into your old programming. It's okay. Just try again. Remember that replacing your disempowering words, which are often instilled in your subconscious, can be a tedious journey. But just like in other things, it can be learned and done with consistency and positive reinforcement.

Now that you're already aware of the steps, let's take a look at some examples of disempowering words that can be turned into empowering ones:

DISEMPOWERING WORDS	EMPOWERING WORDS
It's too hard.	It's challenging, but I can do it.
I'm not lucky.	I create my own opportunities.
I can't.	I can find a way.
I'm not good enough.	I'm worthy and capable.
I'm a failure.	I'm learning and growing.
It's not my fault.	I'm responsible for my actions.
I have to.	I choose to.
I'll never be able to do it.	I am willing to learn and improve.
I should do it.	I will do it.
I don't know how.	I'm willing to learn and ask for help.
I'm stuck.	I have the power to change.
I'm not important.	I am of great worth and value.
I don't have time.	I will make time for what's important.
I'm too old/young.	It's never too late/early to start.
It's just not my forte/talent/skill.	I'm capable of anything I set my mind to.

Empowering Words for Effective Communication

Just imagine if one of the two people speaking always has disempowering words running through his mind. How would he respond to the messages he receives? It could be likely that instead of trying to understand the other person, he might focus on his own weaknesses and failures which will impact his reaction and the way he receives and interprets the information.

Now what if both persons are used to uttering disempowering words in their heads? Well, there's a great likelihood that they won't be able to communicate effectively. Let's say they're working side-by-side on a project. If one frequently thinks "It's not my talent and I can't do it" and the other one often thinks "I'm not good enough and I don't have time", what do you think will happen? They probably won't achieve their goals or it might not turn out so well. Furthermore, in the process of planning and getting closer to their goals, they may fail to work harmoniously or delegate tasks efficiently. They may end up blaming or complaining, or not progressing at all.

Now using this example, let's take a look at the other side of the coin. What if both of them have empowering words for themselves? One always says "I'm capable of anything and I can learn this" while the other one frequently repeats the words "I'm certainly worthy to lead this and very capable, and I can make time for it because it's important." In this scenario, there's a very good probability that they will cooperate with one another and communicate their ideas and plans effectively. Their positive energy can be contagious too, which can lead both of them to have superb ideas and fantastic action plans. Furthermore, if they're leading a team, they can create a positive vibe among the people. This can thus lead to greater productivity and better results.

How about another example? This time, let's take a look at a married couple. If the woman always thinks "I should do it" because she feels obligated to dedicate her entire life to her family, then she might end up not being happy and just keeping her sentiments to herself. If her husband keeps thinking "It's not my fault" that she's unhappy, he is stripping himself of the chance to turn around the situation and make her happy. They may not be able to arrive at a compromise when they have such disempowering thoughts in their heads. On the other hand, if the wife says "I will do it" then this signifies a decision with her consent and willingness. Therefore, she'll be more happy to perform such tasks. She must then communicate to her husband what things she's really happy to do for him. And if the husband starts to change his thoughts too, he might begin to think "I'm responsible for my actions and partially for what's happening to our marriage". As a result, he can assess the situation and pinpoint the things he can change or adjust in order to compromise and make his other half happy. In addition, he too can communicate his needs effectively while paying attention to his wife's needs.

In the examples given above, it's very clear how empowering words can help mold us into more effective communicators. Such words or phrases can foster positive emotions and help us become more attentive, thoughtful and understanding toward others. It can also help build trust and rapport, as well as enhance problem solving, which we've seen in the given situations.

Empowering words can help create a more supportive environment and can assist in developing collaboration and productivity in various settings and groups.

Section 13: Use Your Physiology to Your Advantage and Improve Your Emotional State

Are you sitting up straight while reading this? Or are you slumped on the chair or maybe lying on your bed? Try these different postures and positions, and see how they affect how you're feeling. It goes to show us that even our physiology can affect our emotional state.

According to the results of one notable study conducted by San Francisco State University researchers and published in the journal called Healthy Psychology in 2017, participants who were asked to sit upright felt more positive and energized as compared to those who were slumped. Furthermore, the upright group also recalled more positive memories. In this research, it's been suggested that the upright posture may have led to increased self-confidence, which in turn influenced mood and memory recall. Another great implication of this study is the fact that such an overlooked aspect like posture can actually help with mood disorders and other similar conditions.

Furthermore, the American social psychologist, best-selling author, and keynote speaker Amy Cuddy, PhD, mentioned in her TED talk that two minutes of "power poses" each day can have a great impact on our emotional state. According to her, a "power pose" means standing in a way that exudes confidence even when we are not feeling confident. If we do this even for two minutes everyday, it can boost our mood and actual confidence, and help us face challenges better. It can also increase our chances of success in life.

So, knowing all this, start putting it into your practice. From now on, sit up straight instead of slumping, apply a confident stride when walking, and stand tall and proud when talking to people. You'll soon discover just how amazing the effects will be on you and your life.

Importance of Physiology

Physiology is defined as the study of the body in relation to stimulants. It aims to examine organisms to understand how they function and react. This is why we have discussed above how the way you sit, stand, walk, and move can affect your emotional state, which causes a spiraling effect. Your emotions can make an impact on your thoughts, words, and actions.

In general, our physiology can have a huge effect on how we feel about ourselves and even about others. It can empower us to fight for our dreams, to overcome difficulties, and to take action even when we are scared or unsure. For example, if you're starting a business and everyday you wake up and smile at yourself in the mirror and stand with confidence as you go about your tasks, it can help you feel like you're already successful. It can put you in the right mindset for growth and success. From there, you'll be more encouraged to act accordingly or to keep pursuing it despite the setbacks.

How does it impact our communication skills? For one, our body movements can give out clues when we are speaking on stage or to others. If you're saying you're interested in what's being said, but your shoulders are hunched and your eyes are droopy, then the body language you are displaying is contrary to your words. It might give a mixed signal to the other person, or cause misunderstanding. For instance, if your spouse is explaining about something and your arms are crossed and your body is tense, they might not believe that you're willing to listen and compromise. They may take it that you're being defensive or unwilling to work it out.

Being an effective communicator means that your body language is aligned with what you are saying and is helping you get your message across clearly. Aside from the nonverbal cues through your body movements and gestures, physiology involves breathing, speech rate, tone of voice, and inflection. All of these things will also affect the way you delivery the message and the way it's received. For example, if you're a teacher who's lecturing on something, but your tone of voice is uncertain or your speech rate is too fast, your students may either not believe in what you're discussing or they just won't understand you. Some may simply choose to tune out. Hence, in this case, you were not an effective communicator. This is why we see here that physiology plays a big role in effective communication.

Moreover, cultural and social norms also affect our physiology and therefore affect our communication too. For instance, in some cultures, people believe in looking straight into the eyes while talking. But in others, this could maybe mean disrespect. In such cases, you'll have to be wary of cultural and social differences and adjust your physiology accordingly.

And as mentioned earlier in this section, a lot of studies have shown how physiology affects the emotional state. Emotions are very important in communication because they can influence the way we compose our message, the words that come out, and how we receive the information being passed on to us. Feelings can get in the way or they can also emphasize the message. They can completely stop a conversation or help it move forward.

Overall, our physiology can have a huge and profound impact on how effective our communication is. We ought to be mindful of how we speak, stand, sit, act, and move around because all of these things can influence our connection with others.

Section 14: Understanding the Basics of Effective Communication

We've been talking about how important it is to know ourselves in order to become very good communicators. And you already got a sneak peek at how the communication process works in the earlier part of this book.

But now, let's dig a little deeper into the basics of communication itself! How did you communicate with your parents about wanting to buy something or go out with your friends? How did you react to your boss's assigned task? How did you update your organization on the project you're handling? All these examples point to the importance of communication skills, which are the abilities that we use to send a message as well as receive them from others.

By learning the basics of effective and powerful communication, we can improve our ability to connect with people and inch closer to achieving our personal and professional goals. In our daily interactions, for instance, we can cultivate more meaningful relationships and foster deeper connections. Just imagine what would happen if you often mess up your messages to others! It would definitely spell disaster.

Being a great communicator in the workplace or in your business can definitely help you perform better and boost your sales. For example, your job is to sell laptops. Or even if you're just a clerk who stamps letters. There will still be instances wherein you'll need to communicate with other people. And if you cannot listen well or communicate your own messages effectively, there's going to be a big problem. When we encounter problems along the way, effective communication can help us navigate tough conversations as well as understand the other person's perspective. Additionally, you get to also express your ideas and opinions clearly without much risk of worsening the situation.

Developing Essential Communication Skills

We've already established that communication skills are highly useful and vital in life. What are some examples of communication skills that you should develop in order to become an effective communicator? Remember that some of these must go hand-in-hand.

Take a look at the basic but important skills below:

Listen actively. Always pay close attention when you're speaking to someone, as this is a sign of respect and it will also allow you to absorb and understand the message clearly. Take away distractions like gadgets and other projects while you're communicating with someone else.

Learn to adapt to the audience. Naturally, different styles of and approaches in communication are necessary depending on the audience. Always consider who you're talking to so you can adapt your language, nonverbal cues, and even the message itself. For instance, you can't talk to your employer the way you talk to a long-time buddy. You can't use slang expressions and cursing when you're in a job interview.

Be responsive at all times. Isn't it annoying when someone doesn't respond quickly, even just to acknowledge what you said or sent? An effective communicator replies fast and doesn't keep the other party waiting long. Again, this is a sign of respect especially if you value the person who sent a message to you.

Show friendliness and confidence. This is also important because being friendly and kind can foster trust and understanding, which are both vital in communication. Simple things like smiling and nodding can go a long way. In addition, when you are communicating an idea with confidence and making eye contact, that is regarded with more value. People will tend to listen more attentively and also be more recipient of what you're saying.

Know how to empathize. Understanding and sharing others' emotions is what empathy is all about. If you become good at this, the conversation will go better. The communication can be more effective because then you will respond better to the other person's emotions, such as when they are angry or fearful or frustrated. You'll understand each other better in the process.

Adjust volume and clarity of your voice. This skill can also work wonders in communication. Have you ever tried talking to someone that mumbles or whispers? It must have been hard to understand them and to provide a suitable response. Always consider the setting, the person, and the situation in adjusting your volume and clarity to be fitting. For instance, you can speak in a softer voice in a fine dining restaurant or speak louder when you're in a concert.

Give and receive feedback. You want to become a powerful communicator? You must also know how to receive criticisms well. It's still feedback, after all, that you can use to better yourself. Make sure too to provide your own input when appropriate. This will enrich the communication and allow more ideas and alternatives for the goal at hand.

Understand nonverbal cues. Communication is more than just the words. In fact, majority of it is made up of the body language, facial expressions, hand gestures, and other nonverbal cues. Be observant and also be conscious so you can avoid misunderstandings.

Be respectful. Respect in communication enables better relationships, which paves the path for better understanding of what the senders really mean. Some examples of showing your respect is to clarify things, avoid interrupting, and stay on topic.

Tips on Improving Communication Skills

Don't worry if you're not yet a strong or effective communicator at present. The skills mentioned above can improve with constant practice and with deliberate training. Here are some ways you can improve your communication skills:

Think before you speak. Make it a habit to pause before opening your mouth, no matter where you are or who you're talking to. It's always good to think about what you want to express before actually saying it. This can help you avoid boo-boo's and potential conflicts.

Be clear and concise. Most of the time, it's best to use shorter and lesser sentences that contain your main message instead of beating around the bush with long ones that may end up confusing the listener or receiver. Make sure to reduce your message to something that's easier to consume.

Stay calm and consistent. A lot of people mess up their communication when emotions get in the way. That could trigger you to use foul language, to confuse the other person, or to end up not saying anything at all. Thus, you must try to remain calm even when you are provoked or stimulated. Also practice consistency with your tone of voice and body language, showing everyone that you are in control of what you are saying or showing.

Be assertive. When there's something you want to request, raise, or react to, go ahead. Assert yourself. It will definitely help improve your confidence and communication skills rather than just accepting everything and staying mum. For instance, if someone is treating you unfairly or you want to make a special request at work or in a restaurant, communicate it!

Jot it down. A lot of experts will tell you that it helps to write down your thoughts and ideas because we might forget even the main points at times. Whether you're in a meeting, about to deliver a speech, or planning to speak to your boss, you can always jot down what you want to say or even while listening to others.

Pay closer attention. Because there are so many stimulants around us every single day, we must practice paying closer attention to what people say to us and even to the nonverbal cues we see from others. This will train us to become attentive listeners and better communicators.

Model an excellent communicator. In everything that we wish to learn, especially if we want to grow in a particular area, it always helps to have a model. Think of the people you interact with, watch live or online or on TV, listen to on the radio, and so on. What aspects of their communication do you like and admire? For example, you can model how they persuade or influence others or you can model how they respond to a disturbing or sensitive piece of information. Check their language and nonverbal cues, and see how they are able to communicate effectively in terms of sending and receiving a message.

Section 15: Leveraging Mentors, Role Models, and Coaches

In many industries, if not all, having a mentor, coach, and role model can help us learn faster and become better in what we are trying to achieve. All of these people play a significant role in providing guidance and enabling us to progress more while avoiding mistakes that they may have committed in the past along the way.

How can we distinguish one from the other? It's important to know the difference among these three type of people. All of them play a crucial role for our success in becoming an effective communicator. Understanding what each one can bring to the table will enable you to determine which of them you need the most in your present situation and which of them is essential at your current level of communication.

What is a Mentor?

A mentor is someone who works with you long-term, giving guidance and advice based on their expertise and experience. This is most likely a person who has personal experience and success in the field where you're asking them to mentor you. Mentors usually talk with you about your dreams and goals, then helps you refine the action plans toward attaining them. Moreover, mentors are also expected to give recommendations on the opportunities and steps you ought to take as well as the potential setbacks you should be aware and suggestions on how to avoid or overcome them. They take this mentoring further and deeper by inspiring you and discussing important things like the underlying reasons you have for pursuing your chosen aspirations. In addition, they may also provide motivational exercises that are tailor-fit for you.

In the field of communication, this mentor will likely help you come up with a plan and timeline on how to become an effective communicator. This could include daily exercises, weekly or monthly exposures to training sessions, and regular discussions on which areas you're progressing at and which ones you need to improve on. Your mentor could possibly ask you to describe why you are so determined to become a better communicator and how you think it will benefit you. At times, your mentor might ask you to imagine yourself as the best communicator in your field or in your community.

What is a Coach?

A coach is someone who works with you on a shorter basis because they are more focused on particular areas or skills. The coach is probably an expert in a certain area where you might need more help or assistance in. Typically, coaches make use of techniques and tools in a more structured way in order to provide learning and guidance in achieving a specific goal.

In wanting to become an effective communicator, you may perhaps hire a coach to teach you to become a better public speaker. In this regard, you may be given a customized training plan on voice projection, body language, pacing, and even coming up with content. The coach can also provide ways on how to deal with stage fright, mistakes, anxiety, and other concerns.

Here's another example: If you have a language barrier that gets in the way of effective communication because English isn't your primary language, for instance, then you could probably get an ESL teacher or coach to help you in this arena.

What if you want to become better at understanding people? This is definitely one area of communication that will boost you to become more effective at it. In such case, you may need the guidance of a people skills coach or relationship coach. These professionals can help you in connecting with different people, building rapport, initiating conversations, and developing good and long-lasting relationships. They may help you focus on active listening, conflict resolution, emotional intelligence, and nonverbal communication.

What is a Role Model?

Think of a person whom you wish to emulate when it comes to effective communication. This person may speak and listen in a way that you admire and would like to imitate. Thus, such people are your role models.

A role model is someone with qualities and skills that you would like to have too. You have great respect for this person and often look at how they behave in specific situations. They could be famous people that you've never met or they could be ordinary people in your life.

Can you think of someone right now that you wish to be your role model in effective communication?

For instance, some people would like to emulate Oprah Winfrey because of her apparent active listening ability, her confidence and authenticity, and how she communicates in a clear and concise manner. Because she's able to connect with others on a deeper, more personal level, and she's also good at capturing her audience's attention, she is considered a very good communicator. What's more, her genuine nature helps build her trust and credibility with people.

You want to expedite your journey and success in effective communication? It would be good to have all these three in your life. They need not be separate people. Your role model could be your mentor. It's also possible that your mentor and coach are the same person.

Leveraging on such professionals can make a big difference. Many experts and successful people continue to utilize them in their careers and lives even when they have already achieved a certain level of success. So whether you're a beginner or you're in the intermediate or advanced level of communicating, having a mentor, coach, and role model will be of great value.

However, in evaluating your current status, you can determine which is the most essential for you at the moment. For example, if there's a specific area that you're concerned about and would really need to improve fast, you can hire a coach for that. Or if you're always losing motivation and really need someone to be accountable for, maybe a mentor would be best for now. Or let's say you don't have the budget yet and you simply want to learn on your own and be inspired constantly, then you could go for a role model in the meantime.

Always keep in mind that leveraging mentors, coaches, and role models will accelerate your growth and path to success exponentially. Without them, it will be like groping in the dark and always doing trial and error. But with these professionals guiding you, you'll move faster toward achievement.

Section 16: Working on Your Credibility and Trust

In today's complex and ever-changing world, establishing credibility and trust is more important than ever before. Imagine if you're a business owner who's trying to promote your products and services, but people know you as a scammer. Do you think they would want to buy from you? What if you're a leader in an organization and you're delivery a speech to the members? If you previously got involved in a scandal that questioned your integrity, do you think the members will still listen to you? Indeed, cultivating a reputation for integrity and reliability is essential for success. However, in a world where misinformation and fake news abound, achieving credibility can often feel like an elusive goal. How do you establish yourself as a trustworthy authority when people are bombarded with conflicting information from all directions? What steps can you take to build a reputation that people can rely on? In the field of communication, it doesn't matter what you're talking about or how good you are in delivering the message. If you are not a credible person and people don't trust you, it's very likely that you'll fail in effectively conveying your message to the receiver.

The Meaning and Importance of Credibility and Trust

What exactly is meant by credibility and trust? Credibility and trust both inspire respect from others. These are qualities that a person has when others believe in them and are confident that they can rely on them.

So how are they different from one another? Credibility is often what comes out of using your head because it stems from track record and evidence. When your leader has been in service for many years and has never violated any policy and has always "walked the talk", they can be seen as credible.

On the other hand, trust is more about the heart. It's based on someone's character and intentions. For instance, if your parents always tell you the truth and have proven time and again that they have good intentions for you, which is the basis for their actions, then you'll likely learn to trust them.

When you're trying to communicate something, being credible and trustworthy plays a major role. No one will believe what you're saying if you don't possess these two important traits. It's not just reserved as a requirement for leaders in various fields, it's also essential when you are in sales and marketing, or in the teaching and training industry. What's more, in personally connecting with different people you meet and interact with, you must also emulate these traits in order to be an effective communicator.

Thus, if you want to truly be effective in communication, you must also work on credibility and trust.

How to Build Credibility and Trust

These are not something you are born with, which means it's both challenging and also a blessing.

Let's take a look at the first perspective. It's challenging because no one is fortunate enough to have these built-in when they come out in the world. As a result, building credibility and trust takes time and consistency and great effort. You must be patient and always aware of your words and actions.

How about the second perspective? Not being born with credibility and trust is a blessing because then you can start from scratch and build your way up. You can begin with a clean slate, choose your words carefully, and make decisions that will make people see how credible you are and that you can be trusted.

Now let's go to the nitty-gritty. How do we go about working on these two very important things?

The first thing you must do is to build character and integrity. In doing so, you have to first determine what your core beliefs and values are. You must know to stand up for them because they are important to you and you believe in them. In addition, you must stick to your promises and make sure that you do the right things for the right reasons — always, and even when no one is looking.

Authenticity is also vital here. There are people whom you know are true to themselves and don't seem to have other things up their sleeves. If your motives are clean and you show people that you do what you say, then it's easier for them to believe in you and to see that you are for real. What you see is what you get.

When it comes to developing your credibility, one requirement is to build your expertise in a particular field. Focus your efforts in order to keep learning and practicing in that specific area, thus later on getting the reputation of an expert.

Furthermore, you must always act professionally. This is shown when you exhibit dedication for your work and respect for colleagues and others. It's also apparent in you when you know how to control your emotions even when they are triggered. A professional is well-mannered and well-dressed too.

Before people can fully trust you and see your credibility, you must also be able to show off good communication skills. This means that when you listen, you do it attentively so you can comprehend what the other person is saying and you can form an appropriate and well-informed response. Strengthen your active listening skills and make sure to stick to the truth.

According to a study conducted in 2014 and submitted during a colloquium of the National Academy of Sciences in Washington DC, if we want to communicate efficiently, trust and credibility must go together. There are some professions and jobs in life that are viewed with more trust, and others that are considered more credible. In particular, the study found out that the public generally believes in the competence of scientists, thus having belief in their credibility. However, scientists are considered of low warmth, which results to a lack of trust.

Using this study to inspire us, we have to therefore strive to build our competence and track record in a certain area so we can gain credibility. At the same time, it's also important to show warmth, build rapport, and sustain good relationships with people in order to gain trust. By doing both of these things, it will definitely boost our chances of becoming better communicators in the long run.

Section 17: Thinking Big

According to American motivational writer and personal development expert and author David Schwartz, we have to "Believe big!" because "The size of your success is determined by the size of your belief. Think little goals and expect little achievements."

Many successful individuals and personal development experts have always said that everything begins in the mind. Those who are able to dream and think big, coming up with a colossal, seemingly impossible vision and backing it up with amazing plans — these are the people who are able to achieve more over the long haul. Why? Because they started by shooting for the moon. They chose not to listen and be thwarted by the "small minds".

It's normal to think small for a lot of people because it's what we have gotten used to. Just try to remember how you felt when you failed after trying for something so big. Remember how your loved ones would remind you to be realistic when you described a huge dream? And do you recall how you were often told by the people around you why you can't do something or that you're not allowed to try something? All of these may not be wrong because they only had good intentions for you. However, these things have piled up over so many years and molded our brains to view "thinking big" as something that's risky, not safe, quite impossible and a waste of time and energy. Hence, numerous individuals grow up and even die without dreaming big and just staying contented with what life throws in their way.

If you take a look at the lives and behaviors of those people who achieved great success, you will realize that it all really begins with thinking big. For instance, Steve Jobs was known for his daring vision and relentless pursuit of excellence. Thus, his innovative ideas enabled incredible milestones in the technology industry. Because of him, revolutionary products like the iPod, iPhone, and iPad came to fruition. Another example is Henry Ford, known for making it possible to produce goods on a massive scale and create affordable cars for everyone's use. There was a time when he'd instructed his engineers to design a V8 engine to be mass-produced too. They told him it was impossible, but he kept on pushing it until they eventually found a way to do it. Ford was therefore credited for the development of the V8 engine, a landmark achievement in the history of automobiles.

Today, we can also look at Elon Musk's example. He is definitely seen as a very big thinker, even to the point that many have called him crazy in the past. Nevertheless, some of his crazy ideas were actually turned to reality! He's known for his bold thinking approach and unwavering determination, which paved the way for him to develop companies like Tesla, SpaceX, and Neuralink.

Don't worry if you're not thinking big right now, or if you feel like the way you dream and think isn't big enough. Here are some ways for you to make yourself a bigger thinker:

Hang out with successful people. Not only will you learn a lot from these people, the way they think will also rub off on you. What's more, interacting with such individuals can inspire you to work and push harder and never give up no matter what challenges come your way.

Expand your mind with books and other materials. When you are a big reader and you also like to fill your mind with learning materials, you expand your perspective. You get to see and learn about worlds that you haven't been to. You learn about the past, other places, and other people, and all of these things help you visualize new things and come up with fresh ideas too. These can do wonders for achieving great things in life.

Learn to visualize. Can you believe it that Walt Disney was fired for lacking creativity? And now look at how his vision of Mickey Mouse and the world of Disney came out to be all over the world! Learn to use your imagination to its full potential, without getting held back by your limited mind and experiences. Visualize the amazing things that you want in life, and feel them as you picture them in your head. You'll be surprised at how opportunities and the right people will suddenly appear in your life to lead you to the reality of that visualization.

Set aside limitations. We are all built with limitations in our heads. Sometimes we tend to think we're too young, too old, not too smart, not too pretty, not too talented. But instead of focusing on these things, why don't we place our attention on the things we can do now and in the future? Limitations are only temporary, and may frequently be based on the current situation. So start thinking up creative ways on how you can get around the limitations.

Always think long-term. When you practice this, then you won't get frustrated easily by setbacks because you know that your vision is big and your timeline is long. There's no such thing as overnight success! So plan for your massive goals throughout a longer period of time, and don't forget to celebrate your small successes too. Thinking long-term will train your brain to keep learning and growing, and looking toward the future. You'll find yourself more willing to sacrifice some things, and more willing to get out of your comfort zone.

Multiply your thoughts and ideas by 10x. What are your financial goals? Multiply those by 10x! What are your relationship goals? Multiply those by 10x! Write them down and describe in detail. Don't succumb to the normal conditioning of thinking small and playing it safe.

In elevating the way you think, you can then come up with ideas and action plans to make it come true. If you don't jack up the goals, then you'll always just resort to smaller ideas and plans.

Go out of your way to explore and discover. Just like with books and other materials that you immerse yourself in, you ought to also get out there and explore the world. The more places you visit, the more cultures you discover, and the more people you visit, the more you'll expand your mind and think bigger! And when you keep engaging in new experiences, it just adds more to the capacity of your brain. In addition, this also means that you have to be willing to give your ideas a try or else you'll never find out where they'll take you.

In thinking big, you'll definitely become more confident and creative. It's like making your brain stretch and exercise regularly! And when you expose yourself to new things frequently — books, places, experiences, people — then that will surely expand your vocabulary and improve the way you communicate. It will be easier for you to shape your message according to who you're talking to. Furthermore, as mentioned earlier in this book, empathy also plays a role in communication. When you're a big thinker, you learn to develop empathy so then you can better understand the needs and perspectives of your audience.

Section 18: The Importance of Embracing Failure

"The deafening silence hung in the room as I stood before a sea of expectant faces. Sweat trickled down my forehead, and my hands trembled uncontrollably. It was a defining moment—a chance to communicate my ideas, influence minds, and leave a lasting impact. But deep down, I knew failure was lurking, ready to pounce."

A lot of speakers have gone through this exact moment, with similar thoughts, right before stepping on stage and addressing their audience. There's always a risk of failure in every endeavor. But then, it's something we must accept in order to grow and learn. It's something we need to embrace, so we can move forward with greater strength and more improved skills.

Failure—the mere thought of it had always struck fear into many people's hearts. The fear of stumbling over words, of being judged, of falling short of expectations. It had held us back, stifling our growth in various aspects of our lives, including our development as effective communicators.

Yet, when we stand in front of others, when we overcome that fear of failure and go through with it even when we are afraid and unsure, a realization shall take root within us —a realization that would change everything.

Embracing failure isn't a weakness; it's a superpower. It is through failure that we discover our true potential and get to unlock our hidden strengths.

At one point or another, you've probably gone through failure. It can look like many different things — being put down by your boss, not finishing a project, encountering financial troubles, getting a divorce, breaking a diet, raising a disobedient child. And it makes sense to feel depressed, disillusioned or frustrated because of these things.

What separates successful individuals from unsuccessful ones is the reaction to failure. Do you detest it and push it away? Or do you embrace it and use it to your advantage?

Embracing failure is very important. It can do wonders for our lives.

One good communicator who embraced failure is the world-renowned billionaire author J.K. Rowling, who penned the immensely popular Harry Potter books.

Before Rowling achieved worldwide fame and success, her journey was fraught with failures and rejections. She experienced numerous setbacks, including the loss of her mother, a difficult divorce, and financial struggles as a single parent. As she pursued her passion for writing, she faced rejection from multiple publishers who rejected her initial manuscript for Harry Potter.

However, Rowling's determination and resilience in the face of failure were instrumental in her eventual success. Rather than allowing rejection to deter her, she used it as fuel to refine her writing and storytelling skills. Rowling embraced failure as an opportunity to learn and grow, and she persisted in pursuing her vision.

Rowling's ability to communicate effectively was pivotal in her journey as an author. She understood the power of storytelling and created a rich and captivating narrative that resonated with millions of readers worldwide.

Moreover, her willingness to discuss failure openly has not only endeared her to her fans but also encouraged others to persevere through their own setbacks.

J.K. Rowling's story demonstrates that embracing failure is integral to personal growth and achievement. By embracing failure, she not only honed her craft as a writer but also developed into a powerful and influential communicator, touching the lives of millions through her words and inspiring them to embrace their own journeys, failures, and successes.

Why Embracing Failure Leads to Success

Try asking the successful people you know how they started and became successful. Surely most of them, if not all, will share with you their struggles and talk about how they overcame the challenges along the way. It's very likely that all of them had gone through failures, but chose to rise again and start over or simply keep going.

Think about how Thomas Edison experimented a thousand times with inventing the light bulb before he got it right, about how Michael Jordan failed to shoot the basketball thousands of times and yet became a popular icon in this sport, about how Mark Zuckerberg faced criticism and controversy with his Facemash project which eventually led him to create the top social media platform Facebook.

All of these people went through an experimentation process, which they would not have done if they hadn't embraced failure. They all knew that they wouldn't get it perfectly the first time. Yet they tried and persisted. They were not afraid to fail because they knew that it's the best path toward eventual success.

Aside from experimentation, another important ingredient for success is self-discovery. In order to become an achiever in any field, you ought to know yourself well. Know your compelling reasons as to why you want to make it big. Know your strengths and weaknesses. Know your vision and analyze your situation so you can make a good action plan. In confronting failure, you can discover a lot of things about you and about your goals and projects and plans. Some of them may lead to detours that you never thought would end up as a better way to get to success. Other things you discover can ignite inspired actions and help you realize what to focus on.

In embracing failure, you are also practicing the growth mindset. This type of mindset, as you've previously learned in this book, is the belief that things can be learned and you can improve over time. It's the belief that mistakes are okay because they teach you to be better. This mindset also teaches us to embrace challenges and try new things which can expand our horizons and open us up to new opportunities. Imagine how having a growth mindset can bring about so many possibilities and allow us to persevere despite the difficulties. Hence, it's the right mindset to have for success. And when you learn to accept and welcome failure, then every time it comes, you learn and grow. You get to level up your growth mindset.

Furthermore, embracing failure also enables us to step out of our comfort zones. It's definitely not comfortable to fail, to try new things, to keep going even after you stumble. Thus, as you keep doing it, you get used to being in your courage zone rather than sticking to what you're comfortable with already. In any industry or area, success requires going out of the comfort zone.

Valuable Lessons Gained from Failure

Don't be afraid to fail. Instead, look forward to it. Why? Because there are so many valuable lessons that we can gain from failures.

Here are some of these amazing lessons:

You will become resilient. The more you fail and get up again, the more you'll develop better mental toughness and resilience. These are both essential components of success.

You will learn to be humble. Failure can teach humility, so that we learn to keep our feet grounded even in the midst of many achievements. This way, people will continue to respect us and find us easy to relate to.

You will know how to take calculated risks. Playing it safe never made anyone successful. There are always risks to take during the journey to success. And when you embrace failure, it means you're willing to take risks in order to get to your dreams and goals.

You will become more empathetic. Just like humility, being empathetic allows you to relate easily with others and to understand them better. In the long run, it's a great way of establishing stronger connections and relationships that will contribute to your overall success.

You will get to realize your weaknesses. It's not enough for us to know what we're good at. It's important to find out our weaknesses so we can work on overcoming and improving them. Not knowing these weaknesses may stop our growth.

You will embrace accountability. Learning to be accountable and not to blame other things for your failures will make you more responsible and will put you in better control of your own future. It's also a good way to eradicate excuses.

You will learn to innovate. Imagine if there was no failure? Then how could the great men and women of history have come up with alternatives and innovative solutions? Some of the best inventions and discoveries in the world emerged from innovations brought about by failures.

Embracing Failure and Becoming a More Effective Communicator

Have you ever observed how you adjust your words and tone of voice when talking to different people? Perhaps some of these adjustments came out of failures in communication.

If you speak more than listen when talking to your friends and they eventually avoided you, then that means you haven't been an effective communicator in your conversations with them. That's a sign for you to improve and to be more alert and sensitive when talking to them.

Let's say you use casual, slang words from your cultural background when talking to your team as their leader. It's hindering both parties from better comprehension. Therefore, you can improve by choosing the right words carefully and making sure to use a language that's more appropriate and easier to understand for the people you're talking to.

Effective communication requires continuous learning and improvement. By embracing failure, you view mistakes as valuable learning opportunities. As shown in the examples above, there's a need to analyze communication failures in order to understand the reasons behind them and to identify areas for improvement. This process of self-reflection and learning can help refine our communication skills while also pushing us to develop new strategies and approaches in conveying a message.

What's more, we should remember that fear of failure often hinders effective communication. People may be afraid of public speaking or expressing their ideas, or even engaging in difficult conversations. Mainly this is due to the fear of making mistakes and being judged. But when we embrace failure, it helps us confront these fears and build confidence. We should accept failure as a natural part of the learning process, so that we'll be more willing to experiment with various communication approaches and also to take risks in taking part in new communication situations. In addition, having this increased confidence will allow us to express ourselves more authentically and to engage with others in a more impactful way.

Here's yet another great thing about embracing failure when it comes to communication — it fosters an open mindset. This means we get to be more receptive to feedback and we learn to adapt and be flexible. As a result, we can adjust the approach depending on the person we're talking to. We can revise the channel of the message or the words and tone used.

Earlier we mentioned that failure teaches us to be humble and empathetic. Indeed it encourages us to develop a sense of authenticity in our communication. When we demonstrate humility and empathy, it's easier to connect and build trust. It's also easier to empathize with others' struggles and to show understanding, making our communication more genuine and relatable.

Lastly, just because you failed to convey a message properly doesn't mean you'll give up having conversations or asserting yourself or initiating communication. As we continue to experience failures, this will entail the development of perseverance. You'll learn to bounce back, handle conflicts, and maintain good and effective communication amid challenging situations.

Section 19: Improving Self-Confidence

No matter how good you are in composing a message and choosing the words to convey an idea, it will not be relayed effectively if you don't do it with confidence.

Having self-confidence will allow you to deliver a message with conviction and clarity, thus convincing the receiver of the authenticity and importance of the message.

This confidence is often accompanied by nonverbal cues such as the way you stand and maintain eye contact, as well as the tone of voice you use.

Just imagine this — would you rather listen to someone whose shoulders are slumped and who's speaking in a soft, uncertain voice or would you rather listen to someone who smiles and looks you in the eye and speaks with credence?

Factors Affecting Your Confidence

In order for us to gauge the level of confidence we have and to understand what we need to work on, it's essential to be aware of the factors that affect our confidence. Here are some of the most common:

Physical Well-Being- Naturally, someone who's not feeling well will not sound confident when saying something. But aside from health and fitness, appearance also plays a big role. When you are dressed appropriately and you know that you've taken care to look presentable, then it helps you be more confident.

Past Experiences- Accomplishments and positive experiences from the past can definitely boost your confidence. But if you've experienced disappointments, challenges, and setbacks, these may have made you feel inferior or fearful, thus hindering your confidence. What you can do is reframe you perspective, focusing more on the lessons and growth opportunities you can get out of the negative experiences. Then set achievable goals, break them down into smaller steps, and be sure to celebrate every little progress.

Emotional State- Just like with physical well-being, it's important to be in a good emotional state for you to speak confidently. For instance, if you've just been through a fight with a loved one, chances are you won't be able to converse effectively afterwards. Your communication might be impaired when emotions get in the way.

Self-Esteem- This refers to how you view yourself, or your self-worth. People who have low self-esteem will surely struggle with confidence. You have to believe in your capabilities and know that you can keep learning and improving so as to increase your self-esteem.

Topic Knowledge- When you're not knowledgeable on a particular topic, it's only normal for you not to be able to muster enough confidence when speaking about it. But if it's something you're familiar with or you've researched it previously, then it will shine through in your communication.

Feedback Received- When it comes to communication, the response you get from others will matter in either boosting or bringing down your confidence. In receiving negative feedback, it's important to clarify what is meant and which exact things led to this input. This way, you can work on improving specific areas. Reach out to people who can support and validate you afterwards. Also remind yourself that this feedback is for a particular behavior or outcome, but doesn't define you or your self-worth at all.

Practical Tips to Improve Confidence

You already know that confidence can impact your present life and your future, both personally and professionally. Hence, you should start working on improving your confidence by doing the following:

Always prepare and practice. Whether you're going for a job interview or you have a meeting with colleagues, make sure to do your homework or research. Prepare for what's about to happen, so you'll feel more confident. Keep putting yourself in situations where you can practice and become a better communicator.

Be an active listener. When listening to others, genuinely engage and pay attention. Also avoid distractions and demonstrate interest and understanding.

Focus on your strengths. When you place your energy on what you're good at and what makes you feel good, you can boost your confidence. You can utilize these strengths to communicate well.

Practice positive self-talk. Of course it's always a good idea to use positive words when talking to yourself. This will put you in a good mood, thereby making you exhibit positive vibes and confidence too. Remember, it all begins in the mind.

Embrace nonverbal communication. Don't just depend on words, but rather also work on your posture and body language so you can exude confidence and make people feel your commanding and positive presence.

Expose yourself to challenges. Little by little, you can level up your activities and the situations you are involved in so that you and your communication skills will gradually be challenged. When you do this, every time you climb a notch higher, you'll feel more confident. It's better than staying stuck, which can eventually make you feel worthless.

Section 20: Practicing Gratitude

Did you know that being grateful can make you feel more alive and put you in a positive mood? What's more, it can do wonders for your health, boosting your immune system and improving your sleep too.

In a fascinating study conducted at the University of Pennsylvania, a remarkable revelation unfolded: the act of penning and presenting a truly heartfelt thank-you letter manifested an amazing effect on the authors themselves. Astonishingly, the recipients of such letters were not the sole beneficiaries of joy, as the writers experienced a profound surge of happiness lasting an entire month. Furthermore, the same group of researchers stumbled upon yet another extraordinary discovery: by merely jotting down three positive events each day for a mere week, individuals managed to elevate their happiness levels to unprecedented heights, defying the constraints of time and maintaining their blissful state for an awe-inspiring six months.

Here's another interesting fact! Scientists who are doing research on positive psychology also found out that an act of gratitude can actually give an immediate 10% increase of happiness and at the same time reduce depression by 35%!

So yes, let's not underestimate the power of gratitude. Go ahead and say a simple "thank you" to someone or give a sincere compliment. A mere smile or hug to express appreciation can certainly have a good impact on the recipient and on you too.

Every single day, you can do little acts of gratitude. Take note of all the blessings in your life, big or small, and write them down in a gratitude journal. You'll be surprised at how it can help you feel so much better and put you in a positive disposition.

Tips and Tools for Practicing Gratitude

In order to develop what we call a Gratitude Attitude, you need to cultivate habits that encourage you to notice little things and new things that you're grateful for everyday. Instead of always reciting that you're grateful for your job, why don't you try to be more specific each day by saying something like, "Today, I'm grateful for the sense of accomplishment from closing a deal with my client" or "I'm grateful that I learned another new skill at work"? Rather than simply repeating that you're grateful for your family, you can write in your gratitude journal, "I'm grateful that my husband cooked for me tonight because I was so tired" or "I'm grateful that my son drew a picture to cheer me up".

Think journaling has become stale? Try being more creative! Draw what you're grateful for instead of writing. Or if you're musical, describe what you're grateful for and turn them into the lyrics of a song! You can also write on pieces of paper to fill up a gratitude jar. Also try having gratitude sessions with people you love and trust.

It's important for us to train our brains to become grateful. All you need to do is pay close attention to the positive things that you receive or have. Someone helped carry your things in the supermarket? Your daughter gave you a hug out of nowhere? You were able to finally finish that project? These are all amazing things we can appreciate in our lives! The more you focus on them, the more they'll appear in your life.

How Gratitude Affects Your Communication

Gratitude helps us grow a positive mindset because our focus is on what we value and appreciate. Hence, as a result, our interactions will also be more positive. You'll be more likely to convey optimism, warmth, and appreciation, and this can certainly create a more engaging and receptive environment for communication. Try it! You'll be surprised at how easier it is to build rapport and to develop mutual respect. Thus, those you communicate with will feel more at ease with you and will likely trust and like you more.

Being grateful also encourages us to be more attentive to others. This helps us develop active listening skills and we'll get to connect with other people on a deeper level.

Here's another advantage of gratitude in communication: you'll have a more positive perspective when it comes to conflicts. Just imagine how you'll be open to dialogue and the opportunity to learn and grow, instead of getting swept away by your raging emotions. Grateful people tend to be calmer and directed toward a constructive solution that would benefit all parties.

Section 21: Integrity Rules

Integrity plays a pivotal role in effective communication, ensuring that our words and actions align with honesty, respect, and authenticity. It is essential to avoid certain detrimental behaviors that undermine integrity, such as the following:

1. Gossiping

When we engage in gossip, it not only erodes trust but also reveals a lack of discretion, making others hesitant to confide in us. For instance, imagine a co-worker spreading rumors about a colleague's personal life or making derogatory comments. This not only damages the reputation and self-esteem of the person being gossiped about but also destroys trust and teamwork in the workplace. It also reflects negatively on the gossiper themselves, who can be perceived as untrustworthy or unable to maintain confidentiality.

2. Judging

Judging others means forming opinions or making assumptions based on limited information. It can hamper open dialogue and connection, as it creates a hostile environment. Examples include body shaming and cultural stereotyping, both of which can hurt others' feelings and damage self-esteem.

3. Negativity and Complaining

Both of these can drain enthusiasm from conversations, leaving participants disinterested and seeking an escape. What if you hear someone at work saying, "I can't believe how much work we have to do, and how little we are paid!" and then you respond by saying, "I know! The workload just keeps piling up, and there's not enough time to do it all!"? This dialogue perpetuates a cycle of negativity, reinforcing the belief that the situation is insurmountable without offering any constructive solutions. Thus, meaningful conversation is stifled and problem solving is not applied.

Upholding our integrity means steering clear of the practices mentioned above. When we demonstrate integrity, it shines through in our communication style and our reactions to others' thoughts and viewpoints. This creates an environment conducive to a vibrant exchange of ideas and perspectives. Moreover, by embodying integrity, we effortlessly cultivate trust and forge stronger connections with those around us.

Section 22: Learning to be More Present

Embrace the power of being present! It's like unlocking a hidden treasure chest of awareness, both within yourself and in the world around you. But hold on, let's face the truth: staying present is no cakewalk. It requires active effort, a deliberate choice to infuse your daily routine and communications with this transformative practice.

Imagine the myriad distractions vying for your attention, constantly tugging at your thoughts. The buzzing notifications, the relentless thoughts, the constant pull of past regrets or future worries. They threaten to sweep you away from the present moment, which can certainly get in the way of effective communication.

Though it may be a challenge, there are ways on how you can create a deeper sense of self-awareness, pay greater attention to what's happening in the now, and develop a remarkable ability to engage with the world in a meaningful way.

Here are some ways you can learn to be more present:

Check in with yourself and appreciate the moment.

Engage your senses and be present. Where are you? What do you see and hear? Feel the world around you. Is there a breeze or sunlight on your skin? Immerse yourself!

Observe others too. What energy do they radiate? Do they seem sad, happy, nervous, excited, scared? How do they interact?

Now, turn inward. How do you feel? Let your emotions shine. Express gratitude for blessings and cherish the small wonders of this moment.

Celebrate little successes and joys in your life.

Have you ever experienced finding some cash in your bag or pocket that you never expected? Have you bumped into a good friend or gotten an unexpected gift? Pay attention to all the little things in your life that you can be happy about and that you can celebrate. Together, they're definitely a big deal! This will teach you to focus on the positive things in the now, instead of worrying too much about the past or future.

Practice mindfulness regularly.

Some people do meditation or yoga. Others read about mindfulness and take on other practices to intentionally improve themselves in this area. If you do it daily, soon it will come naturally and make you more present!

Be a great listener.

Sometimes, we tend to think about what we want to say next during a conversation instead of just concentrating on listening actively without the intention of responding. It's best to listen with curiosity rather than always anticipating something. People will surely appreciate you for it and they'll feel like you're really interested in what they have to say.

Be in tune with your feelings.

Release the grip of over-analysis and the urge to alter your emotions. Instead, do embrace a practice of observing your feelings without judgment. Reject the notion that certain emotions are negative and that perpetual positivity is the only path. Just allow yourself to experience and acknowledge your feelings as they arise.

Say goodbye to distractions.

The majority of us seldom live in the present moment, constantly besieged by distractions. Our attention may briefly land on one task, but swiftly a new thought, demand, or duty captures our focus and leads us somewhere else! Take a moment to recognize your sources of distraction — digital devices? stress and anxiety? Then craft a strategy to avoid them. For example, set designated periods of time each day to use your phone and laptop. Prioritize self-care and engage in activities that bring you joy and relaxation. Or start and end your day with mindful breathing exercises.

Learning to be in the present moment is essential too to becoming an effective communicator. When we are fully present, we listen attentively, observing not only the words being spoken but also the nuances of non-verbal cues. It also helps us respond genuinely and in an empathetic way, leading to better understanding and connection. We become attuned to the needs and emotions of others, and thus can adapt our communication style accordingly.

Being present allows us to focus on the conversation at hand, avoiding distractions and truly engaging with the speaker. This heightened presence enhances our ability to convey our thoughts, ideas, and emotions with clarity, authenticity, and impact, ultimately strengthening our communication skills.

Section 23: The Importance of Active Listening and Humility

Did you know that active listening involves being humble? In every conversation we have, it's very important to listen well. To do this, you don't necessarily need to always nod and agree. It's more about engaging, which is a big sign of humility, as you are willing to understand the feelings and perspective of others without interrupting or arguing.

Someone throws something negative toward your direction, saying bad words or criticizing your opinion? Relax and try to stay calm. Always seek to understand first before reacting. Yup, it's challenging, but this is what humility is all about.

Another way to practice active listening with humility is to repeat what's being said so that you can make sure that you're getting the message right before you respond. You can even ask questions for clarification and better understanding!

Want to become an effective communicator? Please listen with an open heart, which will translate to body language that shows you are willing to pay attention and give importance to the other person.

What else? You ought to avoid interrupting. Be sure to think carefully of your response before uttering it. Doing so can enhance your listening skills and show people that you are humble and respectful, thus drawing them closer to you and making you more efficient in communication in the long run.

| Part 3 | Crafting the Message

Section 1: Mental Models and Framework Thinking

Introduction

Ever been amazed by those folks who always seem to have the perfect answer, effortlessly handling questions on the spot without breaking a sweat? You might've thought it was all about their sky-high IQ, but guess what? We can actually train our own brains to think fast and respond in a flash too! In this section, we're gonna explore the one thing that can get your brain in tip-top shape, primed for lightning-fast thinking before you even open your mouth.

First principles reasoning, breaking down problems into their most fundamental truth

Reasoning from first principles, rather than by analogy, involves breaking down complex ideas or problems into their most fundamental truths or basic elements and building understanding from there. It is a method of thinking that seeks to uncover the underlying principles and assumptions behind a concept or situation, rather than relying on previous knowledge or comparisons to similar situations.

When you reason from first principles, you start with fundamental facts or self-evident truths and then use logical deduction and critical thinking to arrive at conclusions. This approach allows you to question assumptions, challenge conventional wisdom, and explore new possibilities.

In contrast, reasoning by analogy involves comparing a new situation or problem to something familiar or previously encountered. It relies on drawing similarities between two things and applying the knowledge or lessons learned from the familiar situation to the new one. While analogical reasoning can be useful for drawing quick associations or making predictions based on past experiences, it may not always lead to accurate or innovative insights.

Reasoning from first principles is often associated with a more rigorous and systematic approach to problem-solving, as it encourages independent thinking and a deeper understanding of the subject matter. By breaking down complex ideas into their fundamental components, you can analyze them objectively and derive new insights that may not be immediately apparent through analogy-based reasoning.

This approach is commonly employed in scientific research, engineering, philosophy, and other fields where a deep understanding of the fundamental principles is essential. It allows for a more comprehensive and creative exploration of ideas, leading to breakthroughs and new discoveries.

➡ **Steer, Don't Follow: Riding the Waves of High-Pressure Conversations**

Navigating conversations can be a daunting task for many individuals who struggle with choosing which route to take. The difficulty often involves grappling with options and trying to assemble a clear direction for discussion. However, there's hope! We can overcome this challenge by learning how to think strategically using frameworks.

Frameworks serve as reliable structures that allow us to arrange our thoughts systematically and pinpoint essential factors crucial for achieving our intended goals. By applying fundamental principles instead of plain analogies we can deconstruct complex theories effortlessly. An excellent example is the revenue framework - calculating income as units sold multiplied by their price. This model enables us to manage financial issues better and decide whether its more effective to raise product prices or push up sales numbers.

➡ Building a Library of Frameworks: A Toolkit for Thought Wizards

The ultimate goal of framework thinking is to create a splendid library of frameworks on the topics that set your heart ablaze. And here's the real magic: by connecting different frameworks, you'll unlock deeper insights and whip up responses that'll knock 'em off their feet! Think of it this way—alongside the revenue framework, you can make friends with the profit framework: profit equals revenue minus cost. By breaking down costs into nifty categories like marginal cost and fixed cost, you can journey further into the realm of increasing those profits.

➡ Leveraging Frameworks in Conversations: Unleashing Your Verbal Brilliance

Once you've built your framework library, it's time to unleash its power in all sorts of situations. When someone comes to you asking how to make more money, you can whip out your trusty revenue and profit frameworks to dish out tailored advice. By assessing their unique circumstances, you can suggest tweaks to the number of units sold, crafty pricing strategies, or even ways to optimize those costs. Frameworks become your trusty compass, guiding you through complex topics with ease, offering insights that'll leave 'em starstruck and recommendations that'll make their jaws drop.

➡ Learning and Creating Frameworks: Mastering the Art of Mental Jujitsu

Now, you won't find frameworks on your typical school syllabus, but fear not, my friend! There are two mighty ways to get your hands on 'em. First up, you can create your very own frameworks. By distilling your knowledge down to its purest essence, you'll create structures that'll whip your brain into a quick-thinking shape. For instance, let's mosey on over to the world of business storytelling, where the ethos-pathos-logos framework (that's credibility, emotions, and logic) can be a nifty tool to analyze the effectiveness of presentations or marketing messages.

➡ Finding Hidden Frameworks: Unearthing Gems of Wisdom

Now, here's a sneaky approach—unearthing those hidden frameworks lurking on the vast internet. Many wise authors have packed valuable information without even labelling it as a framework. But fear not, by organizing that treasure you'll create frameworks you can easily reference. Take the concept of "ikigai" in Japanese culture, for example. It's all about finding the purpose of your life and can be a trusty framework for making money while doing what you love. Break it down into its four elements—what you love, what you're good at, what you can be paid for, and what the world needs—and voilà! You've got a ready-made framework to tackle all those related questions.

➡ Building Your Framework Library: A Treasure Trove of Mental Marvels

If you wanna be a quick thinker, focus on building a breathtaking library of frameworks that sing to your heart's desire. Connect 'em like puzzle pieces, and suddenly, you'll find yourself comfortably exploring a wide range of topics. Armed with direction and knowing which levers to pull, you'll unlock profound insights and uncover hidden gems of analysis. Sharing the frameworks we use every day can light up the path to collective wisdom!

➡ Conclusion

Training your brain to think fast and respond with flair in conversations is within your mighty grasp. All you gotta do is embrace a framework-based approach. By organizing your thoughts into snazzy frameworks and building a treasure trove of these little marvels, you'll have all the information you need at your fingertips, ready to dazzle the crowd.

Rock Your Presentations: Frameworks for Clear Thinking and Captivating Communication

➡ Introduction:

In the exciting realm of idea sharing and storytelling, we've got some killer frameworks that'll level up your presentations like never before. Here, I'm gonna hook you up with presentation frameworks that'll supercharge your communication skills. Get ready to captivate your audience and make an impact that's off the charts!

➡ The Information-Entertainment Scale

Alright, let's dive into the big daddy of frameworks: the Information-Entertainment Scale. This bad boy helps you find that sweet spot for your presentation. We're talking about the perfect balance between informative and entertaining, tailored to your goals and your audience's taste.

Purely informative presentations? Picture news broadcasts or snooze-inducing lectures. Yeah, they can get real dry and boring, my friends.

Purely entertaining presentations? Think stand-up comedy or show-and-tell sessions. These babies are all about engaging and amusing your audience but don't expect 'em to leave with a truckload of knowledge.

Now, the sweet spot: edutainment presentations. These puppies strike that perfect balance between info and entertainment. You're dishing out valuable insights while keeping your audience glued to their seats.

➡ Choosing the Perfect Position for Your Presentation

When it comes to picking your presentation's spot on the Information-Entertainment Scale, you've gotta consider two crucial factors: you and your audience.

Executives on the clock? You better believe it. When you're presenting to busy company big shots, like those management consulting honchos, efficiency is the name of the game. They want concise, evidence-backed recommendations that'll help 'em make quick, informed decisions. Impress these folks, and you'll open doors to future collaborations.

Teaching the young guns? Oh yeah, this one's a balancing act. You gotta serve up the goods, but make it fun, my friends. Students need a mix of information and entertainment. Keep 'em engaged, make 'em laugh, and they'll walk away with those juicy takeaways.

Everybody wants a good time? If both you and your audience are craving an entertaining presentation, it's time to borrow from the comedians. Whip out those frameworks they use for killer wedding toasts or hilarious skits.

➡ Presentation Frameworks

Alright, here's where the magic happens. Let me break down some kickass frameworks that'll take your presentations to the stratosphere.

Pyramid Principle for Informative Presentations

Let's start with the OG, the Pyramid Principle. This gem helps you share information like a pro. We're talking concise and compelling delivery. Here's how it goes:

1) Cut to the chase: Start with your conclusion, the big kahuna. Boom! Hit 'em with that main point or answer right off the bat.

2) Back it up: Now, support that conclusion with three strong arguments. Give 'em the meat and potatoes, people.

3) Show 'em the evidence: If needed, back up each argument with three pieces of rock-solid evidence. We're talking undeniable proof, my friends.

By following the Pyramid Principle, you're setting a clear goal, anticipating their questions, and knocking their socks off with a focused and impactful presentation. Boom!

Curiosity Gap for Mixing Entertainment with Information:

Alright, let's mix things up a bit. Enter the Curiosity Gap framework. This baby will grab your audience's attention and never let go. Here's how it rolls:

1) Get 'em curious: Start by introducing the topic, but hold back on revealing the answer or main idea. Leave 'em hangin', my friends.

2) Make it relevant: Show 'em why this topic matters, why they should care. Give 'em that "aha" moment, and watch 'em lean in.

3) Deliver the goods: Finally, promise 'em value. Let 'em know what they'll gain or learn from your mind-blowing presentation. Hook, line, and sinker!

By using the Curiosity Gap, you'll have 'em on the edge of their seats, begging for more. They won't even know what hit 'em. Bam!

Rate of Revelation for Entertaining Presentations

Alright, buckle up for the Rate of Revelation framework. This one's all about timing, my friends. You gotta control that information flow to keep 'em hooked. Here's the deal:

1) Need for speed: If you wanna amp up the excitement, drop those intriguing and mysterious bits of info like rapid-fire. Keep 'em on their toes, craving more.

2) Slow and steady: If suspense is your game, take it slow. Reveal those details bit by bit, building that delicious anticipation before dropping the bomb. Boom!

Both approaches have their charms. Fast rate of revelation is perfect for gripping narratives and storytelling, while the slow rate builds that tension, leaving 'em hanging on your every word.

Effective communication and presentations demand structure and flawless delivery. And with these killer frameworks, you'll be a communication mastermind. You'll enhance your ideas, engage your audience, and leave 'em in awe. Remember, communication is an ongoing adventure, and by embracing these frameworks, you'll level up your presentation skills like a boss. Now go out there, rock storytelling, idea sharing and presentations, and leave 'em begging for more.

➡ Considerations on Simplicity & Clarity

To achieve effective messaging; clarity and simplicity are key elements in today's fast-paced world of communication. Simplifying a complicated message into bite-size pieces helps it get through amidst all the noise by eliminating fluff and complex terms which can be difficult to decipher by an audience. Meanwhile, clarity leaves no room for misinterpretation by being an unambiguous ray of understanding projected to the audience.

Deploying both powerhouses facilitates a betters connection between your ideas and your audience while streamlining decision-making for them. Greetings reader! To ensure seamless delivery of your message; keep an eye on structure (thinking in framework) because – let's be real- nobody wants to get lost along the way! Clear paths lead to cohesive comprehension so opt for headings and visual aids designed specifically for this purpose, they're immensely helpful as guides facilitating ease of retentive learning in audiences. Your most reliable tool towards mastering communication involves seeking feedback from openly communicative allies– make sensible notations from reliable input whilst addressing areas that require attention aiming towards "constant improvement" before relaying information. Progressing simplicity and clarity are vital – let's trade in complex terms for streamlined focused thoughts with a solid structure that resonates with audiences!

Section 2: Examples of Frameworks to get you started

Frameworks are like supercharged tools that help you understand and make sense of complex subjects in all sorts of fields. They provide a structured way of thinking, organizing information, and solving tricky problems. Now, the list of frameworks we're going to dive into isn't exhaustive, but it's a fantastic starting point to show you just how awesome and versatile frameworks can be across different disciplines.

Believe it or not, frameworks are everywhere! Whether you're exploring physics, economics, business, psychology, or sociology, you'll find these powerful frameworks at work. They offer invaluable insights, principles, and models that help you analyze, explain, and navigate through the mind-boggling complexities of the world around you.

By embracing frameworks, you gain clarity, connect the dots, and dig deeper into complex subjects. Whether you're a student, a professional, or just a curious explorer of the world, frameworks will unlock new insights, supercharge your understanding across different disciplines and help you communicate more effectively!

Economics

➡ Supply and Demand

Supply and demand is about how the availability of something (supply) and how much people want it (demand) determine its price. When something is in high demand but low supply, its price tends to go up. Conversely, when something is in low demand but high supply, its price tends to go down. For example, if there is a limited supply of a popular toy during the holiday season, its price might increase.

➡ Cost-Benefit Analysis

Cost-benefit analysis helps you make decisions by comparing the costs and benefits of different options. You weigh the advantages (benefits) against the disadvantages (costs) to determine if something is worth doing. For example, if you're considering buying a new gadget, you would think about the cost of the gadget and the benefits you would gain from using it to decide if it's a good investment.

➡ Comparative Advantage

Comparative advantage is about specializing in what you do best and trading with others who specialize in what they do best. It recognizes that different countries or individuals have different strengths and weaknesses. By focusing on what they are relatively better at producing, they can trade with others and benefit from each other's expertise. For instance, if one country is good at growing bananas and another country is good at manufacturing cars, they can trade bananas for cars and both countries will be better off.

Psychology

➡ Maslow's Hierarchy of Needs

Maslow's Hierarchy of Needs is a theory that explains human motivation. It suggests that people have different needs arranged in a hierarchy, starting from basic physiological needs like food and shelter, to safety, belongingness, esteem, and self-actualization. The theory proposes that individuals fulfill their lower-level needs first before moving up to higher-level needs. For example, you need to satisfy your hunger and have a safe place to live before you can focus on building relationships or pursuing personal growth.

➡ Cognitive Biases

Cognitive biases are shortcuts or patterns in our thinking that can lead to errors or irrational judgments. These biases can affect how we perceive information, make decisions, and interpret events. For example, confirmation bias is the tendency to seek information that confirms our existing beliefs and ignore evidence that contradicts them. Being aware of these biases can help us make more rational and objective judgments.

➡ Behaviorism

Behaviorism is a psychological approach that focuses on observable behavior and how it is influenced by environmental factors and consequences. It suggests that behavior can be learned through conditioning, either through rewards or punishments. For example, if you train a dog to sit by giving it a treat every time it sits, it will learn to associate sitting with the reward and be more likely to sit in the future.

Relationships

➡ Love Languages

Love languages refer to the different ways people give and receive love. It suggests that individuals have different preferences in how they feel loved, such as through words of affirmation, quality time, acts of service, receiving gifts, or physical touch. Understanding each other's love languages can help improve communication and strengthen relationships. For example, if someone's love language is acts of service, they may feel most loved when their partner helps them with chores or tasks.

➡ Conflict Resolution

Conflict resolution styles are different approaches people take to resolve conflicts. Some common styles include avoiding conflicts, accommodating or giving in to the other person's needs, competing or asserting one's own needs, compromising to find a middle ground, or collaborating to find win-win solutions. Each style has its strengths and weaknesses, and the most effective approach depends on the situation. For instance, if you and your friend have a disagreement, you may choose to compromise by finding a solution that partially satisfies both of your needs.

Business & Strategy

➡ SWOT

SWOT is a framework used to assess the strengths, weaknesses, opportunities, and threats of a business or a situation. It involves identifying internal factors (strengths and weaknesses) and external factors (opportunities and threats) that can impact the success or failure of a business. By evaluating these factors, businesses can develop strategies to leverage their strengths, address weaknesses, capitalize on opportunities, and mitigate threats.

➡ Porter's Five Forces

Porter's Five Forces is a framework used to analyze the competitive forces within an industry. It considers factors such as the bargaining power of suppliers and buyers, the threat of new entrants, the threat of substitutes, and the intensity of competitive rivalry. By understanding these forces, businesses can assess the attractiveness and profitability of an industry and make informed strategic decisions.

➡ Business Model Canvas

The Business Model Canvas is a visual tool that helps entrepreneurs and businesses map out their business model. It consists of key elements such as customer segments, value propositions, channels, customer relationships, revenue streams, key activities, key resources, key partnerships, and cost structure. The canvas provides a holistic view of the business and facilitates strategic thinking and planning.

➡ PESTEL

PESTEL is an acronym for Political, Economic, Social, Technological, Environmental, and Legal factors. PESTEL analysis is a framework used to assess the external macro-environmental factors that can impact an organization's business environment. Each factor is examined to understand its potential influence on the organization's strategies and operations. PESTEL analysis helps organizations identify opportunities and threats arising from the broader socio-political, economic, technological, and legal landscape in which they operate.

➡ Value Chain Analysis

Value chain analysis involves mapping out the activities and processes that add value to a product or service, from raw material sourcing to customer delivery. This framework helps organizations identify areas of competitive advantage and potential cost savings, allowing them to optimize their value chain and develop effective strategies.

➡ Blue Ocean Strategy

Blue Ocean Strategy focuses on creating uncontested market spaces, or "blue oceans," where organizations can differentiate themselves from competitors and create new demand. This framework encourages organizations to pursue innovation, value creation, and market disruption rather than competing in existing market spaces, or "red oceans."

➡ Ansoff Matrix

The Ansoff Matrix offers strategic options for growth by analyzing product and market expansion. It presents four growth strategies: market penetration (selling existing products in existing markets), market development (entering new markets with existing products), product development (developing new products for existing markets), and diversification (entering new markets with new products). This framework helps organizations identify growth opportunities and make informed strategic decisions.

Finance

➡ Time Value of Money

The time value of money recognizes that the value of money changes over time. It means that a dollar received today is worth more than a dollar received in the future due to the opportunity to earn interest or returns on investment. For example, if you have the choice between receiving $100 today or $100 a year from now, you would choose to receive it today because you can invest it and potentially earn more money.

➡ Risk and Return

The relationship between risk and return states that higher potential returns are usually associated with higher levels of risk. When making investment decisions, investors need to consider the potential return they can earn compared to the level of risk they are willing to take. For example, stocks generally offer higher potential returns but also come with a higher level of risk compared to government bonds, which offer lower potential returns but are considered less risky.

Sociology

➡ Social Stratification

Social stratification refers to the division of society into different layers or strata based on factors like wealth, occupation, and social status. It leads to unequal distribution of resources, opportunities, and privileges among different social groups. For example, in a society with social stratification, individuals from higher social classes may have more access to education, healthcare, and power compared to those from lower classes.

➡ Functionalism

Functionalism is a sociological perspective that views society as a complex system with interrelated parts that work together to maintain stability and harmony. It emphasizes the functions or purposes of social institutions in maintaining social order. For example, education serves the function of imparting knowledge and socializing individuals, while the economy provides the means for the production and distribution of goods and services.

Technology

➡ Technology Adoption Lifecycle

This framework explains the stages that individuals and society go through when adopting new technologies. It includes innovators, early adopters, early majority, late majority, and laggards. Understanding this framework helps businesses and innovators plan their technology adoption strategies.

➡ Disruptive Innovation

Coined by Clayton Christensen, this framework describes how new technologies or innovations can disrupt existing markets and industries. It explains the concept of sustaining innovations and disruptive innovations, and how established companies can be caught off guard by disruptive technologies.

➡ Technology Readiness Levels (TRL)

This framework is used to assess the maturity and readiness of technologies for implementation. It provides a scale from 1 to 9, where TRL 1 represents basic research, and TRL 9 represents full deployment and commercialization. TRL helps in evaluating the technological feasibility and risk associated with adopting new technologies.

Marketing

➡ Marketing Mix (4 Ps)

This framework includes product, price, place, and promotion, which are the key elements of a marketing strategy. It helps businesses in designing and implementing effective marketing campaigns and understanding the various components that contribute to successful marketing efforts.

➡ Customer Segmentation

This framework involves dividing a market into distinct groups of customers based on their characteristics, needs, and preferences. By understanding different customer segments, businesses can tailor their marketing strategies and offerings to better meet the specific needs of each segment.

➡ AIDA

AIDA stands for Attention, Interest, Desire, and Action. This framework explains the stages a consumer goes through in the process of making a purchasing decision. It helps marketers in designing persuasive communication and marketing campaigns to guide consumers through these stages and ultimately drive them to take action.

➡ 4Cs Marketing Mix

The 4Cs framework offers an alternative perspective to the traditional 4Ps (Product, Price, Place, Promotion) marketing mix. It emphasizes customer-centricity and includes the following elements:

Customer: Understanding the needs, preferences, and behaviors of the target customer segment.

Cost: Assessing the overall cost to the customer, including not only the purchase price but also other costs such as time and effort.

Convenience: Ensuring that the product or service is easily accessible and convenient for customers.

Communication: Creating effective and relevant communication strategies to engage and connect with customers.

Environmental Science

➡ Ecological Footprint

This framework measures the impact of human activities on the environment by assessing the resources consumed and waste generated. It helps in understanding the sustainability of our lifestyle choices and guides efforts towards reducing ecological footprints.

➡ Life Cycle Assessment (LCA)

LCA is a framework used to assess the environmental impacts of a product or process throughout its entire life cycle, from raw material extraction to disposal. It helps in identifying areas of environmental concern and finding ways to minimize negative impacts.

➡ Environmental Impact Assessment (EIA)

EIA is a systematic process for evaluating the potential environmental effects of proposed projects or policies. It considers various factors such as air quality, water resources, biodiversity, and social impacts. EIA aids in decision-making by providing information on the potential environmental consequences and suggesting mitigation measures.

Education

➡ Bloom's Taxonomy

This framework categorizes learning objectives into different cognitive levels, ranging from lower-order thinking skills (remembering, understanding) to higher-order thinking skills (analyzing, evaluating, creating). It helps educators design instructional strategies that promote critical thinking and learning at various levels.

➡ Constructivism

Constructivism is an educational theory that emphasizes active learning and the construction of knowledge through personal experiences and social interactions. It suggests that learners actively build their understanding of the world by connecting new information to existing knowledge and experiences.

➡ Multiple Intelligences

This framework, proposed by Howard Gardner, suggests that intelligence is not a single entity but a combination of different types of intelligences, such as linguistic, logical-mathematical, spatial, musical, bodily-kinesthetic, interpersonal, intrapersonal, and naturalistic. Recognizing and catering to diverse intelligences can enhance the effectiveness of teaching and learning.

Cultural Studies

➡ Cultural Dimensions

This framework, developed by Geert Hofstede, identifies cultural dimensions that influence behavior and values in different societies. Dimensions such as individualism vs. collectivism, power distance, uncertainty avoidance, and masculinity vs. femininity help in understanding and comparing cultural differences across societies.

➡ Intersectionality

Intersectionality is a framework that recognizes how multiple social identities (such as race, gender, class, and sexuality) intersect and interact to shape individuals' experiences and social structures. It highlights the interconnectedness of various forms of oppression and privilege and promotes an inclusive and intersectional understanding of social dynamics.

Health and Wellness

➡ Social Ecological Model

The social ecological model is a framework that considers the multiple levels of influence on health and wellness. It recognizes that individual health is influenced by factors at the individual, interpersonal, community, and societal levels. Understanding these influences helps in developing comprehensive health promotion strategies.

➡ Biopsychosocial Model

The biopsychosocial model is a framework that acknowledges the interconnectedness of biological, psychological, and social factors in health and wellness. It recognizes that health outcomes are influenced by biological processes, psychological factors (such as thoughts and emotions), and social determinants (such as social support and socioeconomic status).

➡ Transtheoretical Model of Behavior Change

The transtheoretical model is a framework that explains the stages individuals go through when making behavior changes. It includes stages such as precontemplation, contemplation, preparation, action, and maintenance. Understanding these stages helps in designing interventions and strategies to support behavior change.

Physics

➡ Newton's Laws of Motion

Newton was a smart scientist who discovered three important rules about how things move. The first rule says that objects that are not moving will stay still unless something pushes or pulls them. The second rule says that when something pushes or pulls an object, it will start to move or change its speed. The third rule says that for every action (like pushing), there is an equal and opposite reaction (like pushing back).

➡ Conservation Laws

There are rules in physics that say some things always stay the same. One rule is that the total amount of energy, which is what makes things work, doesn't go away or magically appear—it just changes from one form to another. Another rule is that when things bump into each other, the total amount of push or pull they have (called momentum) always stays the same.

➡ Electromagnetic Theory

Electricity and magnetism are like a pair of friends—they are connected! When you use electricity, like when you turn on a light bulb, it creates a special kind of force called a magnetic field. And when you have a magnet, it can make electricity flow in wires. These two things work together and make cool things happen, like the radio and the TV working.

Section 3: Understanding your Listeners and Audience

Understanding your audience ain't just important, it's the very foundation of effective communication. You might have a well-crafted, articulate message, but if it don't strike a chord with your audience, it'll fall flat as a pancake. The key to connecting with your listeners lies in the art of researching. You gotta dig deep and uncover invaluable insights to tailor your message to their needs, desires, and interests. It's like embarking on a thrilling journey of discovery, peeling back the layers that make your audience who they truly are. In this chapter, we're gonna explore a series of steps that'll guide you through the process of researching your audience, giving you the tools and understanding to communicate in a way that grabs 'em and speaks right to their hearts. So, let's buckle up and set off on this transformative journey together, unlocking the secrets to understanding your audience like never before.

➡ Get a Handle on the Demographics

Demographics are the basic facts about your audience. You gotta think about stuff like age, gender, education level, cultural background, and occupation. This info helps you get a better grasp of who they are and what they like. For instance, if you're talkin' to a bunch of young professionals, you might wanna use modern lingo and examples that really resonate with their generation. On the flip side, if you're dealin' with older folks, it's best to stick to more traditional language and references.

➡ Get a Glimpse of Their Values and Beliefs

To really connect with your audience on a deeper level, you gotta understand their values and beliefs. Dig into their interests, affiliations, and check out their social media profiles. This'll give you insight into their perspectives and help you frame your message in a way that lines up with their values and speaks to their beliefs. For example, if your audience is all about the environment, highlight the eco-friendly aspects of your message.

➡ Size Up Their Knowledge Level

Figurin' out where your audience stands in terms of knowledge on the topic you're discussin' is crucial. Are they beginners, folks who know a bit, or experts? Understandin' their level of understanding helps you figure out how complex your communication should be. If they ain't familiar with jargon or technical terms, don't use 'em. Instead, provide clear explanations and definitions so everyone can keep up and get the main points.

➡ Get a Bead on Their Needs and Interests

To grab your audience's attention, it's crucial to address their needs and interests. Run surveys, do some interviews, or dig into existing data to get insights into their concerns and desires. This research will help you shape your message to directly tackle their needs and show 'em that you understand their situation. For example, if your audience consists of managers, focus on givin' 'em practical strategies and solutions to up their leadership game.

➡ Take Notes and Learn from Past Interactions

If you've had previous dealings with your audience, take some time to mull over those experiences. Think about their reactions, questions, and how engaged they were. Were they pumped and involved, or bored outta their minds? By analyzin' these observations, you can get some valuable feedback to improve your future communication efforts. Adjust your approach based on what worked well and what didn't in the past to create a more effective communication strategy.

➡ Make the Most of Online Research Tools

In this digital age, online research tools can give you a treasure trove of insights about your audience. Social media platforms like LinkedIn or Facebook can spill the beans on their professional background and interests. Make the most of these platforms to gather data and gain a deeper understanding of what they prefer. Plus, online surveys and analytics tools can help you collect feedback and measure audience engagement, givin' you solid numbers to shape your communication strategy.

➡ Get Feedback Straight from the Horse's Mouth

Don't be shy about askin' for feedback directly from your audience. After a presentation or meetin', ask 'em what they thought and if they got any suggestions. Their feedback is pure gold for gettin' a sense of their perceptions and it helps you make adjustments for future interactions. And don't forget, encourage 'em to ask questions during your communication to keep things clear and engaging. Actively seekin' feedback shows that you're committed to understandin' and meetin' their needs.

Remember, researchin' your audience is an ever-evolving process. As you connect with different groups, keep honin' your understanding of their preferences, needs, and interests. By investin' time and effort into researchin' your audience, you'll be armed to communicate effectively, build stronger bonds, and deliver messages that hit 'em right in the feels.

Section 4: The Importance of Distinguish Facts vs Opinions

In a world flooded with all sorts of info and different opinions flying around, we gotta know how to separate facts from opinions if we wanna communicate effectively. Whether we're chatting, arguing, or sharing info, understanding this difference is crucial. So we're gonna dig into why it's so darn important to tell facts apart from opinions to boost our communication skills and have more meaningful interactions.

Understanding the Difference

Let's start by clearing up what we mean when we say "facts" and "opinions." Facts are those objective statements you can prove with solid evidence. They're like the universal truths that ain't swayed by personal perspectives. For example, "The Earth orbits the Sun" is a fact we can scientifically back up. On the flip side, opinions are all about those subjective expressions based on personal beliefs, feelings, or interpretations. They're like our individual viewpoints, not something everyone can agree on. Like when someone says, "Blue is the most beautiful color," that's purely their opinion.

The Importance of Distinguishing Facts from Opinions in Communication

➡ Boosting Clarity

When we make it crystal clear what's a fact and what's an opinion, we provide accurate info that others can easily understand. Mixing up the two just leads to confusion and makes our messages less effective. Facts act as solid data points that everyone can agree on. By sharing facts, we can pass on info that's universally accepted and acknowledged. Others can then base their understanding and actions on reliable info. But opinions, well, they're all about personal perspectives and interpretations. While they're great for expressing individual views, we gotta remember they might not hold the same weight or be true for everyone.

➡ Building Trust

Trust is a big deal in communication. When we back up our statements with well-supported facts, we establish ourselves as reliable sources of info. That builds trust and confidence in what we're saying. But when opinions get mistaken for facts, it messes with our credibility and makes people doubt the accuracy of what we're saying. So, to strengthen our street cred, we gotta make sure the info we present is backed by solid evidence. Facts give us that solid foundation. We can support them with scientific research, historical records, expert testimonies, or fancy stats. By clearly stating when we're dropping facts, we show we're committed to accuracy and being reliable. That makes others trust what we say.

➡ Avoiding Confusion

Misunderstandings happen a lot when opinions get treated like facts or the other way around. But if we're aware of the difference, we can reduce the chances of confusion. When we clearly say we're expressing an opinion, others know it's just our personal perspective, not some ultimate truth. That sets the stage for open and respectful dialogue. See, when opinions are passed off as facts, things get muddled, and people can get all mixed up. It's especially important when decisions or actions are based on the info we give. So, by clearly labeling opinions as opinions, we leave room for other viewpoints and encourage others to share their own. That makes communication more inclusive and collaborative.

➡ Finding Common Ground

When we're in discussions or debates, separating facts from opinions helps us have more constructive convos. Facts provide a starting point we can all agree on, which makes for productive exchanges. Opinions, on the other hand, are subjective and differ from person to person. Recognizing that opinions are just personal views encourages active listening and understanding. It opens the door for exploring diverse perspectives and finding common ground. So, by knowing the difference between facts and opinions, we set the stage for meaningful discussions. Facts act like reference points we can all use to analyze and make decisions. They create a shared understanding. Opinions, well, they add flavor to the convo by reflecting our unique experiences and values. When we appreciate that opinions are subjective, we can have conversations that seek to understand and respect different viewpoints. That's how we build consensus and tackle problems together.

Tips for Distinguishing Facts from Opinions in Communication

➡ Watch Your Words

Be careful with the words you choose to indicate if you're talking about a fact or an opinion. Phrases like "Research shows that..." or "According to the experts..." let folks know you're bringing in some solid facts. But if you drop lines like "In my experience..." or "I reckon that...," it's clear you're sharing an opinion. The language we use plays a big role in showing the difference between facts and opinions. When we're stating facts, we gotta use language that shows they're based on objective info. We can mention trustworthy sources or research findings to back up what we're saying. When it comes to opinions, we should use language that lets folks know we're speaking from our own perspective. That way, they understand it's not some absolute truth, just how we see things.

➡ Back It Up

When you're sharing facts, back 'em up with evidence, references, or examples. That makes your message more credible. And when you're expressing opinions, explain the reasons or values behind your viewpoint. That helps folks understand where you're coming from without mistaking it for a fact. To separate facts from opinions, we gotta support what we say with proper evidence. Facts are based on solid data or info that can be confirmed by others. When we bring in scientific studies, historical records, or fancy stats to back up our statements, we show we're grounded in reality. Opinions, though, are based on personal beliefs and interpretations. They're influenced by things like experiences, values, or feelings. So, when we share opinions, it helps to give context and explain the reasons behind our viewpoint. That way, folks get that it's just our personal take on things, and it helps 'em appreciate different perspectives.

Listen Up and Ask Questions

When you're having a convo, really listen to what others are saying and ask questions if something ain't clear. Encourage folks to point out if they're talking about facts or opinions. When we all understand the difference, we lay the groundwork for effective communication. Listening is key when it comes to communicating effectively. In a conversation, it's important to let others fully express their viewpoints. When we actively listen and ask questions to clarify things, we show respect for their perspectives and open up the dialogue. If someone says something that's kinda fuzzy and it's unclear whether it's a fact or an opinion, it's crucial to ask for more details. That helps us better understand what they're getting at and gets us all engaged with the topic at hand.

Section 5: The Rule of 3

When it comes to connecting and engaging with others, it's all about transforming ourselves and keeping it real. In this section, we will be unleashing the power of authentic communication. We'll expose the limitations of mere tips, and I'll give you a framework to build a deep connection with your audience.

Tips, Limitations, and Snoozefests

Tips can give you some insights into communication techniques, but they often fall short in forging meaningful connections. Just following them like a robot—varying your speech pace and volume—can make you sound like a snoozefest, failing to engage your audience. Yeah, those prescribed movements and pauses might look good on paper, but they don't capture the natural flow of conversation and genuine human connection.

The Heart of Connection

Real communication comes from truly connecting with the people you're interacting with. It's about feeling the vibes and getting in sync. When you tap into your own thoughts and empathize with your audience, magic happens. You'll naturally pause, speed up, or raise your voice. It's like a dance, where you and your listener groove together, setting the stage for impactful changes in your speech.

No Overthinking, Just Feeling

Tips often make us overthink the connection we're trying to establish. But they should be more than just items to check off a list. Authentic communication should flow from the connection itself, with tips just being an extension of that connection. No rigid rules, just a natural and flexible approach.

Embrace the Three Rules of Three

Now, even though we should be wary of relying solely on tips, there are three guidelines that I personally find super helpful—I call 'em the "Three Rules of Three." Once you've built a strong connection, these rules can work wonders for effective communication:

Rule of Three Important Points: When you're chatting with others, limit yourself to three important ideas. Keep it focused and clear, so they remember what you're saying. If you have more points, squeeze 'em into this framework. Remember, simplicity is key.

Rule of Three Perspectives: Got a complex concept to explain? Break it down from three different angles. Give your audience a 360-degree view, so they can grasp it better. It's like wearing different glasses to see the whole picture.

Rule of Three Repetitions: Some stuff is just tough to grasp. So, repeat it three times throughout your talk. Each time, it sinks in a bit more, until it's stuck in their heads. Take it slow and steady, and watch their understanding grow.

The Transformation Process

Remember, these three rules aren't just tips, they're part of a transformative process. Think of it like going to the gym, except it's way more fun. You're honing your skills to connect with others, whether through words or writing. It's all about unleashing that innate human ability to connect on a deeper level.

The Joy of Genuine Connection

Now, you might hesitate at times, but let me tell you, connecting with an audience is a pure joyride. When you genuinely enjoy those connections, tips become second nature. You effortlessly apply the principles of effective communication, without even thinking about it. It's like breathing—natural and satisfying.

To become a communication rockstar, you gotta go beyond tips and embrace a transformative approach. Build real connections with your audience and rock the Three Rules of Three—share three important points, tackle ideas from three perspectives, and repeat tricky concepts three times. So, let's kickstart this journey, discover the thrill of connection, and experience the deep satisfaction of engaging with others in a truly meaningful way.

Section 6: The Power of Articulating Your Thoughts

If you wanna be a communication pro, you gotta know how to talk the talk. Being able to articulate yourself effectively is key in all kinds of situations, from chit-chat with your pals to boss-level meetings. In this section, we'll dig into why being a smooth talker matters in different communication contexts and how it can seriously boost your game.

When you've got the gift of gab and can express yourself like a boss, amazing things happen. First off, you'll get your ideas across crystal clear and avoid any major misunderstandings. Plus, being a smooth talker helps you build stronger relationships 'cause people dig that open and honest communication vibe. Oh, and here's the best part: when you can talk the talk, you exude confidence and credibility, and that's gonna make people sit up and take notice.

This section is gonna spill the beans on how to level up your articulation skills in different communication situations. We'll break down the basics of talking right, share tips on making your message clear and convincing, give you the lowdown on adapting your style for different contexts, show you how to practice and polish your skills, and even let you in on how being a smooth talker can skyrocket your career and personal relationships.

So, if you're ready to unlock your true potential and become a smooth talkin' superstar, buckle up and get ready to take your communication game to a whole new level!

Understanding the Nitty-Gritty of Talking Right

When it comes to effective communication, you gotta nail the basics, my friend. We're talking about the importance of being crystal clear, building up your vocab game and mastering grammar and sentence structure.

➡ Getting Your Thoughts Across with Clarity and Precision

No more beating around the bush! Clarity and precision are the name of the game when it comes to articulation. You wanna make sure your ideas hit the bullseye and leave no room for confusion. Expressing yourself clearly means no fuzzy or vague language. And hey, being precise means choosing the right words that capture exactly what you wanna say. Trust me, it'll save you from those "Huh? What did you mean?" moments.

➡ Boosting Your Vocab Power

Words, my friend, are your secret weapons. The bigger your vocabulary, the better you can express yourself. So how do you pump up your word bank? Dive into reading, have juicy conversations, and dig up new words like a treasure hunter. But hey, it's not just about collecting fancy words. You gotta practice using them in the right context, so they roll off your tongue naturally and hit the bullseye every time.

➡ Mastery of Grammar and Sentence Structure

Grammar might sound like a snooze fest, but trust me, it's the glue that holds your sentences together. You wanna make sure you're grammatically on point. No more cringe-worthy sentence blunders. By mastering grammar, you'll sound like a smooth talkin' pro. And hey, don't forget about sentence structure! When your ideas flow like a river, people can follow your train of thought without getting lost in the wilderness.

Clarity, precision, vocabulary, grammar will be your secret weapons for expressing yourself confidently and connecting with others. Get ready to rock the communication world!

Making Communication Crystal Clear

Let's talk about how to make your communication crystal clear! We'll explore some killer strategies to enhance clarity in your conversations. We're talking about organizing your thoughts, keeping it simple and concise, avoiding fancy jargon, spicing it up with examples and anecdotes, and actively seeking feedback. Get ready to level up your communication game!

➡ Organizing Your Thoughts

Before you start spilling the beans, take a hot sec to organize your thoughts. Get 'em all in order, like tidying up a messy room. This helps you stay on track and prevents you from going on a wild tangent. You can jot down main points or create a mental roadmap to keep things flowing smoothly. Trust me, a little organization goes a long way.

➡ Keep It Simple and Snappy

Use language that even your grandma can understand. No need for all that complicated jargon and technical mumbo-jumbo. Break it down for your audience using plain and clear words. Straightforward and concise language gets the job done without causing any head-scratching confusion.

➡ Leave the Jargon at the Door

Here's a pro tip: leave the jargon at the door. Unless you're talking to a bunch of experts in your field, skip the fancy terms. They just make things unnecessarily complicated. If you can't avoid using technical terms, explain them in plain English so everyone can follow along. Remember, clarity is the name of the game.

➡ Sprinkle in Examples and Stories

Let's spice things up! Sprinkle in some juicy examples and stories to make your message pop. Concrete examples bring abstract concepts to life and make 'em easier to grasp. And who doesn't love a good story? Anecdotes and narratives captivate your audience and help them relate to what you're saying. So, don't be shy—share those real-life tales!

➡ Seeking Feedback and Clearing Up Confusion

Communication is a two-way street. Don't forget to seek feedback and clarify any confusion. Encourage questions and actively listen to what others have to say. If there's any fuzziness or misunderstandings, address them head-on. By being open and interactive, you'll deepen the understanding and keep that communication crystal clear.

The Art of Persuasive Communication

Persuasive communication is must have skill for anyone who wants truly meaningful conversations or wants their message out there. It takes intuitive insight into peoples' perspectives to leave mutual interest solutions. Learning how requires following these four significant steps:

1) Approach communication as a way to connect with your audience by understanding what they desire and showing how your idea can appeal to them in an equally impressive manner. 2) Expect and address any objections or criticisms confidently with easily understandable facts. This shows you thoughtfully analyzed the situation before delivering a message.

3) Start crafting your argument by using logic consistently throughout to increase its weight. Start with premises that can be supported by reliable evidence and build up from there.

4) Draw on creative storytelling tactics to expand upon important messages; memorable teachings are often more appreciated when they are delivered within memorable contexts.

Practicing these components for persuasive communication will not only allow you to make exemplary connections but will assure that your message is received in the best light possible!

Persuasion is an art - it means crafting language carefully to influence others effectively. To make our point-of-view accepted often requires some savvy strategy; such as posing thoughtful questions or stirring up heart-tugging sentiment for memorable impact.

One particularly effective weapon in this arsenal of persuasion is telling a story - painting vivid pictures in the minds of those who hear it and leaving them spellbound through chapters of compelling plot lines about heroic characters . Masterful storytellers know how to create scenes that come alive so strongly listeners can almost smell the scent of roses on desert winds (or salty sea air depending on setting), cry when our protagonists get hurt – laugh when something funny happens - they leave us feeling moved more frequently than not!

With these potent tools at hand - deep understanding of the audience we address; focusing on answering questions beforehand; developing strong ideas with perfect arguments at-the-ready;

deploying all-out persuasive flourishes combined with breathtaking storytelling techniques - we'll be unstoppable!

Adapting for Different Communication Contexts

To communicate effectively. One must be adaptable to various communication contexts. Here we will explore techniques for tailoring communication in different contexts, including conversations with friends and acquaintances workplace interactions and professional settings, business presentations and public speaking, networking events and social gatherings as well as considerations for cross-cultural communication. As we engage in conversations with friends and acquaintances it is often appropriate to use a casual and familiar tone. Being authentic helps foster a comfortable environment where we can express ourselves naturally. Active listening allows us to establish meaningful connections. While sharing personal experiences and cracking humor can make the interaction enjoyable.

In professional settings. Clear and concise communication is key. For effective workplace communication. One must be mindful of the audience and tailor language and mannerisms accordingly. Emphasizing professionalism by using appropriate terminology while maintaining a respectful demeanor can contribute to successful interaction. Collaborating with others while actively listening leads to teamwork that propels progress forward; offering constructive feedback contributes to outcome facilitation.

When giving business presentations or public speaking engagements clarity of message is of utmost importance; capturing the listeners attention from the start helps ensure interest as content is shared in an organized manner accompanied by effective visual aids. To enhance effectiveness further engaging a presentation through eye contact while varying vocal tone would also assist in persuading your audience members toward your perspective.

Networking events or social gatherings require approachability; showing genuine interest might establish lasting connections through active listening asking questions through an open ended conversation setting might result in common ground establishment or increased awareness concerning cultural norms that could enhance efficient nonverbal cues like body language involving maintaining eye contact play an equally significant role.

Lastly when participating in cross cultural communications avoiding misunderstandings requires the recognition of cultural norms as well as familiarization with customs and methods of communicating. Effective cross-cultural interaction depends upon adapting one's method of communicating towards clarity while also maintaining an awareness of nonverbal cues.

An individual who aims for openness towards diverse perspectives shows a willingness in learning about varied cultures that cultivate mutual understanding between people from distinct backgrounds. Therefore; taking time out for learning about various cultures is essential

Being successful in a variety of situations necessitates adjusting one's own communicative style according to the context at hand including adaptation based on tone, languages, and outreach towards our audience. A flexible approach leads us towards effective communication which in turn results into building deeper relationships and understanding across diverse cultures and contexts.

Practicing and Refining Articulation Skills

Practicing and refining your articulation skills is key to becoming an effective communicator. Here we will dive into some killer strategies that will help you level up your articulation skills, like getting involved in speaking exercises, rocking role plays, seizing public speaking opportunities, joining communication-focused groups or clubs, recording and reviewing your own speeches, and teaming up with a mentor or communication coach.

So, let's kick things off!

You know what they say—practice makes perfect! Engaging in regular speaking exercises and role plays is where the magic happens. Think of delivering speeches, taking part in mock conversations, or even diving into heated debates. By actively speaking your mind and expressing your thoughts, you'll boost your clarity, confidence, and knack for articulating ideas like a boss.

Now it's time to shine in the spotlight! Public speaking and presentations are prime opportunities to work on your articulation skills. Whether you're speaking in a formal setting or just hanging out with a bunch of folks, embrace those chances to speak your heart out. It's a surefire way to build up your confidence, refine your delivery techniques, and deliver messages like a pro. Trust me, stepping up to the plate will pay off big time!

Why not join the cool kids' club? Communication-focused groups or clubs, like Toastmasters International, provide a supportive and structured environment for honing your articulation skills. You'll get to flex your public speaking muscles, receive some top-notch feedback, and learn from seasoned pros. Surrounding yourself with like-minded folks will keep you on your toes and give you a solid foundation for kicking butt in communication.

Time to hit that record button! Recording and reviewing your own speeches or conversations is a nifty way to assess yourself. By listening or watching yourself, you can pinpoint areas that need improvements, like clarity, pronunciation, or even nonverbal cues. It's all about figuring out your strengths and weaknesses, so you can focus your practice and refine those killer articulation skills.

Don't go it alone, buddy! Team up with a mentor or communication coach who'll have your back. These gurus will provide you with personalized guidance, constructive criticism, and killer exercises that suit your needs. They'll show you the ropes of voice modulation, body language, and overall presentation skills, taking your articulation game to new heights. Having a mentor or coach is like having a secret weapon in your pocket.

By incorporating these strategies into your routine, you'll be actively practicing and refining your articulation skills. Keep up the speaking exercises, seek out those public speaking gigs, join the communication-focused groups, review your recordings, and don't forget to team up with a mentor or coach. Trust me, it's all about continuously improving those articulation abilities, and you'll be rocking it in no time!

Articulation Skills to Improve Career Prospects

Let's talk about how articulation skills can skyrocket your success and take your career to new heights. Whether it's nailing interviews, acing resumes and cover letters, handling tricky workplace situations, building professional relationships and networks, or climbing up the leadership ladder.

First things first, interviews are make-or-break moments, right? When it comes to snagging that dream job, effective communication is the name of the game. Clear articulation, concise answers, and active listening are the keys to making a killer impression. Those rockstar articulation skills will make you stand out from the crowd, show off your value, and prove that you're the one who can make a real impact on the organization.

But it doesn't stop there! Articulation skills go beyond speaking. When it's time to craft your resume and cover letter, you've gotta articulate your experiences, skills, and achievements in a way that makes 'em say, "Wow!" Keep it snappy, highlight those killer accomplishments, and tailor it all to the job you're after. That's how you present yourself as the superstar candidate.

Now, let's dive into the wild world of the workplace. Tricky situations pop up all the time, but with killer articulation skills, you'll handle them like a pro. Express your ideas, concerns, or feedback with clarity and respect, and watch conflicts melt away. Diplomatic articulation, active listening, and finding common ground are the secret weapons to successful communication and problem-solving in the workplace.

Building professional relationships and networks is all about articulation skills. Engage in meaningful conversations, listen actively, and express yourself with clarity and empathy. That's how you build trust and rapport. When your articulation game is strong, you'll have those valuable connections and a network that'll take you places!

Articulation skills are an absolute must for leadership and management roles. Convey your vision, goals, and expectations with precision to inspire and motivate your team. Leading meetings, delivering killer presentations, and articulating strategies like a boss will boost confidence in you. Nail those articulation skills, and you'll be on the fast track to career advancement.

By honing your articulation skills in all aspects of your career, you'll open doors to success. Rock those interviews, ace your written materials, handle workplace challenges like a champ, build professional relationships and networks that last, and climb up that leadership ladder. It's all about articulating your thoughts and ideas like a true pro!

Strengthening Personal Relationships through Articulation

In the realm of personal relationships, being a true listener is like opening the door to their soul. It's about tuning in, not just with your ears, but with your heart. As you lend an ear, you show that you truly care and grasp the depth of their feelings and perspectives. That's how trust takes flight, and your connection soars to celestial heights!

Now, let's face the dragon—conflicts, they breathe fire, don't they? But fear not! Your weapon of articulation can tame even the fiercest of beasts. Speak your truth, boldly and honestly, and watch as conflicts surrender to understanding. Replace blame with understanding, ignite dialogue like a symphony, and marvel at the victories of compromise and harmony. The journey to resolution awaits, where needs unite and friendships are fortified.

Ah, the symphony of emotions and needs, the language of the heart! When you master the art of expression, you paint vibrant landscapes of intimacy and fortify the foundation of your relationships. With words as your brush, vividly share your feelings, desires, and expectations. As your innermost self finds voice, bonds deepen, and emotional well-being blossoms like a kaleidoscope of blooming flowers.

Now, let's unlock the doors of growth and transformation. Offering feedback and criticism is a delicate dance, where words wield the power to uplift and inspire. Paint a picture of growth with your observations, focusing on the canvas of actions instead of tearing at the fabric of the soul. Offer guidance, like a gentle breeze guiding a ship, and watch as bridges are built and relationships ascend to new heights.

When someone you cherish triumphs, it's time to throw confetti into the air and shout from the mountaintops! Shower them with accolades, honor their achievements, and let your words set the stage ablaze with admiration. Through your heartfelt articulation, let them bask in the spotlight.

Unleash the power of your articulation and witness the transformation of your personal relationships. From the enchantment of active listening and empathy to the alchemy of conflict resolution, the poetry of expressing emotions and needs, the magic of constructive feedback, and the jubilation of celebrating achievements—these are the ingredients for a symphony of connections. Now, go forth and let your words dance upon the winds of connection, in the realm of relationships, true magic awaits!

Section 7: Tips on Delivering Your Thoughts

In today's fast-paced world, being a smooth talker can make all the difference in getting your ideas noticed. It ain't always the brainiacs with the best ideas who get the spotlight. Nah, it's them folks who know how to express themselves like a boss.

➡ Trick #1: Kick It Off with a Quote

You wanna grab attention from the get-go? Start things off with a bangin' quote that hits the bullseye. No need for a bunch of pointless jabbering at the beginning. Dive right in and engage your peeps. And hey, using a quote from some legit sources? That'll make you look like a rockstar, 'cause you're rollin' with the big dogs. This trick's sets the stage for a positive and open discussion.

➡ Trick #2: Visuals That Pack a Punch

Don't sleep on the power of visuals! Pick visuals that'll knock their socks off. Show 'em the contrast and changes in a way that makes 'em go, "Whoa!" Break down those complex ideas with visuals that'll make 'em say, "I get it now!" Studies show that folks process visuals way faster than plain ol' text. So, not only will they remember your content better, but you'll also deliver it like a pro.

➡ Trick #3: Finish Strong with Action

When you're wrapping things up, don't leave 'em hangin'. End with a bang! Give 'em an action item that's gonna stick in their minds. But here's the trick: keep it simple, keep it real. Make sure it aligns with your main message. If you're talkin' about fightin' climate change, don't go all complicated on 'em. Just suggest somethin' like bringin' reusable bags to the store. People like easy, and when they commit to somethin' simple, they're more likely to follow through.

To be a communication whiz, you gotta be organized and know your audience. These tricks we've talked about? They're gonna level up your game. Start strong with a quote that catches their ear. Use visuals that pack a punch, makin' your ideas crystal clear. And don't forget to end with a solid action item, makin' sure your message sticks like glue. Remember, it ain't just about what you say, it's how you say it. So, go ahead, embrace these tricks, and watch your communication skills skyrocket!

Section 8: The Best Storytelling Techniques

The basic technique

Picture this: It's August 28th, 1963, in Washington DC, USA. A crowd, mostly African-American, gathers, fueled by a mix of anger and excitement. Discrimination still runs rampant, but they're eager to hear their hero, Dr. Martin Luther King. As he takes the stage, he grabs their attention with immortal words, expressing his dream of equality and justice for all. But let's face it, even with brilliant content, a speech can fall flat if it's not delivered right.

So, here's the deal: Many speeches are snooze-fests that fail to keep folks engaged. As a speaker, your mission is to hold their attention throughout. Now, let's be real, attention naturally drifts away over time. If you don't address that, your audience's interest will dwindle. The secret sauce lies in using techniques that repeatedly grab their attention throughout the presentation.

The power of questions

First up, let's talk about the power of questions. Picture this: You pepper your presentation with thought-provoking questions that don't demand answers but get folks thinking and engaged. Then there are answered questions—ask a question and answer it yourself, smoothly transitioning to the next topic. And let's not forget interactive questions, where you ask the audience something and expect a response. This keeps everyone on their toes and involved. Dr. King himself was a master at using questions to captivate and involve his audience, so you know it's legit.

The power of storytelling

Now, hold on tight because we're diving into the power of storytelling. Picture this: You weave compelling tales that stick in people's minds and tug at their heartstrings. Stories help folks remember stuff and make your speeches hit 'em right in the feels. By spinning yarns, you bridge topics, showcase real-life examples, and make your content relatable.

Oh, and let's bust a myth while we're at it. Storytelling ain't just for certain topics—it works like magic in anything, even the nerdy technical ones. Stories breathe life into dry subjects, making 'em accessible and interesting.

Now, let's break it down. Here's a simple format that'll knock their socks off:

1)Start by laying out the problem you're tackling. Paint a vivid picture using storytelling to show how you personally encountered the problem and hammer home its importance.

2) Dig deep into the underlying causes of the problem. Share stories of your quest to uncover the root issues.

3) Present a range of solutions, backed up by stories that highlight both the wins and the failures.

4) Wrap it up with your top-notch solution or recommendation. Share stories of how it's been implemented and the positive impact it's had.

This format weaves together a killer narrative that guides your audience, keeping 'em engaged and helping 'em remember the juicy details.

The real power of nailing speeches lies in your ability to share your unique message and ideas with the world. When you master the art of public speaking, you gain confidence and create opportunities for your ideas to make a real difference. When you captivate your audience and get your message across, everyone comes out a winner. By sprinkling techniques like questions and storytelling into your presentations, you'll wield a powerful tool for change, making sure your ideas hit home.

The Pyramid Principle Explained

Barbara Minto, a former McKinsey pro, spilled the beans about The Pyramid Principle in her book, The Minto Pyramid Principle. Let me tell ya, it's a game-changer when it comes to problem-solving and how we communicate ideas. Anyone can benefit from it, believe me.

Now, why is this principle so dang important? Well, it's all about structured thinking. Having a solid structure can save your hide during a nerve-wracking presentation with big-shot executives. It helps you present your ideas crystal clear, boosting your confidence levels. Ain't that what we all want? To sound confident and make snappy decisions?

Now, let's dive into how this Pyramid Principle works, shall we? It's all in the name, my friend. Your presentation should have a pyramid-like structure. Start with the grand idea, the core message, and then break it down as you go along.

First things first, hit 'em with the answer, the core message. Keep it simple, snappy, and effective.

Next up, logically group, sort, and sum up your supporting arguments. Each argument should look like a mini-pyramid, if you catch my drift. Ideally, you wanna have three strong supporting arguments. Why three, you ask? Well, it's a magic number. Easy to remember and it keeps you focused on the most important points. When you stick to three, you sound like a pro, all organized and ready to rock.

Once you've made your points, you can dive into the nitty-gritty, the supporting facts and figures. It could be actual data or in-depth analysis. Oh, and here's a little trick I've found helpful: toss in some testimonials to back up your big idea. People eat that stuff up, trust me.

Simplicity is the name of the game when it comes to the Pyramid Principle. Your foundation is the hard data and facts that support your arguments. Once you've laid that out, it's time to level up and think in broader terms. Move up the pyramid at each level until you reach that core message, my friend.

But hey, here's a heads-up. Like everything else, the Pyramid Principle ain't gonna work in every situation. It's a no-go for leave-behind decks or docs. Those usually follow a different approach, bottom to top. And it's not the best fit for data-heavy presentations and deep insights.

In the wise words of Barbara Minto, "Controlling the sequence in which you present your ideas is the single most important act necessary to clear writing. The clearest sequence is always to give the summarizing idea before you give the individual ideas being summarized. I cannot emphasize this point too much."

So, there you have it. The lowdown on The Pyramid Principle.

12 Game-Changing Storytelling Techniques

According to research studies, presenting information in a structured way makes it stick in the audience's minds 40% more than unstructured data. That's a solid fact right there! A good presentation or speech follows a natural flow, with a clear beginning, middle, and end, along with smooth transitions and signposts to guide the audience and keep them engaged. But structuring a presentation ain't no walk in the park; it takes guts and consideration for a whole bunch of factors. You gotta think about your objective, where you'll be delivering your talk, the audience's knowledge level, and even time constraints.

Now, if you're scratching your head, wondering how to organize your thoughts, we've got some mind-blowing ways to structure your speech. So, let's dive right in, shall we?

1) Situation-Complication-Resolution: This structure is killer when you want to persuade your audience. You start by setting the scene, describing the current situation and all its nitty-gritty details. Then, you hit 'em with the complication or problem, really making them feel the impact. But fear not! You come in as the hero with the solution, laying out the steps, resources, and time needed to solve the problem. And to top it off, paint a vivid picture of the benefits that await once the problem is resolved. Throw in some real-life examples, proof, and hard facts to spice things up!

2) Hook, Meat, and Payoff: this structure is all about reeling your audience in and leaving 'em hungry for more. You start with a killer hook—something surprising, mind-blowing, or maybe even controversial—that grabs their attention and makes 'em sit up straight. Then, you dish out the meat of your presentation, the juicy stuff they need to know. And finally, you serve up the payoff, the big revelation or realization that connects back to your hook. It's like a tasty sandwich with all the fixings!

3) Situation-Opportunity-Resolution: You know what they say: every problem's got an opportunity just waiting to be seized. With this structure, you shift the focus from fear to aspiration. Lay out the situation, crystal clear and no-nonsense. Then, shine a spotlight on the golden opportunity that's just begging to be snatched up. And of course, wrap it all up with the resolution—the solution to that pesky problem. Give 'em evidence, proof, and maybe even a dash of swagger to boost your story's credibility.

4) The Drama: Time to unleash your inner storyteller and bring some serious drama to the table! This structure is perfect for showcasing the epic journey of success, whether it's a business triumph or an individual's rise to fame. Picture this: You start with a so-so situation, nothing too fancy. But then, bam! The challenge smacks your hero right in the face, and things start spiraling down, reaching rock bottom. But wait, there's a glimmer of hope—the discovery that sparks belief in solving the problem. Cue the rise, where the hero overcomes the challenge and opens up a whole new world of possibilities. And don't forget the lesson, the big takeaway that your hero learns along the way. It's like a Hollywood blockbuster!

5) The Pitch: If you're out to sell your idea and convince the audience it's the bee's knees, this structure is your go-to. You start by sizing up the current situation, laying it all out on the table. Then, you dive into the hurdles and obstacles standing in the way. But fear not, because you've got the solution up your sleeve. Back it up with data, research, experiments—the whole shebang. And when you reach the close, present the best option as the ultimate problem-solver. Oh, and sprinkle in a little hook, an extra cherry on top of your solution. They won't be able to resist!

6) The Explanation: Time to educate and enlighten! This structure is all about providing information-rich presentations, whether it's about a new regulation, insights, or a fancy new process. You start by giving 'em the lay of the land—where things are now and where they need to be. Then, you whip out the roadmap, a visual guide showing how to get to that final destination. Step by step, you lead 'em through the journey, making sure they understand the why and the how at each stage. Finally, you unveil the grand transformation at the end. It's like taking 'em on an adventure they won't forget!

7) Fact and Storytelling: Time to get a little zigzaggy. This structure deviates from the traditional linear approach and adds some flair to your storytelling. You bounce back and forth between "how things were" and "how things will be," building momentum as you go. It's all about ending on a high note!

So, here's the deal: A well-structured speech can leave your audience informed, inspired, and begging for more. It keeps you on track, boosts your confidence, and ensures your message hits home. So, choose the right structure that resonates with your audience, emotionally and intellectually. And hey, if you're crunched for time or need a little extra pizzazz, grab yourself a pre-designed, high-definition template to give your information that polished, structured look.

8) Freytag's pyramid: Back in 1863, a clever German author named Gustav Freytag did some fancy research on popular plays and came up with a model that stuck around. We call it Freytag's pyramid. According to old Gustav, any story worth its salt has five key parts.

First up, we got the Exposition, where all the important background info is dropped on ya. It sets the stage, so to speak.

Next, we got the Rising Action, a series of events that build up the excitement, leading us to the juicy climax. That's the part where things really hit the fan, the most thrilling bit that gets your heart pumpin'!

After the climax, we ease into the Falling Action. It's like the action keeps goin', but it's windin' down from that peak.

Finally, we wrap it all up with the Dénouement. It's fancy French for the ending, where we tie up loose ends and reveal the resolution, a catastrophe, or a mind-blowing revelation.

You'll see this fancy-schmancy framework used in countless brand videos.

9) Three-act structure, which is like a shorter version of the five-act deal. This one's more popular in short content like social media posts. It's got three key parts.

First, we got the Setup. That's where you set the scene and introduce your main characters, like paintin' a picture for the audience.

Then comes the Confrontation or "Rising Action." It's when a problem pops up or tensions start to build. You can feel the heat risin'!

And finally, we reach the Resolution. It's the sweet moment when all the problems get solved, and everything's hunky-dory again.

10) Donald Miller's StoryBrand framework. It's deceptively simple. It helps figure out the audience (The Character) and their biggest pain point or problem. Then, they become The Guide who'll show 'em the way and solve that problem (The Plan). And of course, there's always a clear Call to Action, showin' The Character what success looks like and warnin' 'em about the tragic outcomes if they choose the wrong (ahem, not your brand's) solution.

11) Pixar Story Framework! This gem was cooked up by Emma Coates over at Pixar. It's become a legend, and you can use it for founding stories, explainer videos, and, of course, Pixar movies. It's based on a few phrases, like a secret recipe.

So, it starts with "Once upon a time there was _____." That sets the stage

Then, every day _____. It's all about what goes on in this character's life on the daily.

But then, one day _____. That's when things take a turn and we're off on an adventure.

Because of that, _____. And because of that, _____. It's like a chain reaction of events, one thing leadin' to another.

Until finally, _____. That's when we reach the grand finale, the big finish!

12) Features and benefits formula. First, you describe the feature. Keep it snappy and cool. Then, you ask yourself, "So what?" to find the benefit. What's in it for your audience?

But don't stop there! Next, you contrast the old way with your new way. Show 'em how you're changin' the game. And here's my special touch: consider who's gonna use that feature and how. Get real details to make the story relatable and inclusive. Then, tell THAT story.

Section 9: Bringing It All Together, A Short Recap

➡ Key Takeaways

- Effective communication is the bee's knees for success in all areas of life
- Communication is a skill that can be honed and improved.
- Mindset and habits are of paramount importance if you want to become a top-notch communicator
- Have a growth mindset and clear goals, and you'll be rocking it. Keep that chin up, manage stress like a boss, and you'll be on your way to effective communication.

- Tailoring your communication style to the audience brings home the bacon.
- Storytelling and structuring is like magic, it keeps 'em hooked.
- Keep it real, authenticity builds trust and credibility.
- Building trust and rapport is the name of the game for effective communication.
- If you wanna nail that speech, you gotta prepare and practice, no ifs, ands, or buts
- Rockin' effective communication means using language like a pro.
- Don't forget, nonverbal communication speaks volumes too!
- Be all ears, ask thoughtful questions, and watch your communication soar.

➡ Closing Notable Quotes

- "The most important thing in communication is hearing what isn't said." - Peter Drucker
- "Communication is not about speaking what we think; it's about ensuring others hear what we mean." - Simon Sinek
- "The way we communicate with others and with ourselves ultimately determines the quality of our lives." - Tony Robbins
- "Communication is the fuel that keeps the fire of your relationship burning. Without it, your relationship goes cold." - William Paisley
- "Your ability to communicate is an important tool in your pursuit of your goals, whether it is with your family, your co-workers, or your clients and customers." - Les Brown

| Part 4 | Delivering the Message

Section 1: Mastering the Voice

When it comes to effective communication, it's not just about the words we choose, but also how we deliver 'em. By employing various vocal techniques, you can enhance the impact and influence of your speech. Whether you're delivering a presentation, engaging in a conversation, or addressing a group, these tools will help you captivate your audience and convey your message with clarity and authority.

Register

One major factor in communication is our vocal register – y'know, the pitch range we use when we speak. Now, if you wanna really nail it, mastering your register can make a world of difference in how you convey authority, power, and presence. In this section, we're gonna dive into the importance of vocal register and give you some practical techniques to harness its power for kick-ass communication.

➡ Understanding register

First things first, let's get a grip on what register is all about. Vocal register is basically the range of pitches we use when we talk. And guess what? It plays a massive role in how others perceive us. When we speak from the chest with a lower voice, we ooze confidence, authority, and credibility. On the flip side, if your voice is higher-pitched, it might not command the same level of authority. But don't sweat it! Once you understand your register and take control of it, you can seriously level up your communication skills.

➡ Developing Chest Voice

Now, let's talk about developing that chest voice of yours. It's all about being aware and taking control. Check out these exercises to help you deepen your voice and speak from the chest like a pro:

First off, <u>breathe</u>. Yup, focus on your breath. Take deep breaths and let that air fill up your diaphragm. Practice exhaling slow and steady, maintaining a constant flow of air. This exercise helps you build up breath support, which is key for projecting a lower and more resonant voice.

Now, let's get <u>humming</u>! Start by humming at a comfy pitch, then gradually lower it while keeping that chest vibration going. Feel those vibrations resonating from your chest area? That's what you wanna go for. This exercise helps you explore and expand your lower vocal range – pretty cool, huh?

Oh, and don't forget about vocal <u>warm-ups</u>! Get your voice in shape by doing some gentle vocalization exercises in your lower register. You can try descending scales or hold out those "oo" or "uh" sounds. Keep at it, and you'll build up that chest voice strength over time.

➡ Utilizing Lower Register in Communication

Alright, now that you've got control over your chest voice, it's time to rock it in your day-to-day communication. Here are some killer strategies to make the most of that lower register:

First off, pace yourself. Speak slowly and deliberately, giving each word and phrase the time it deserves to resonate. This deliberate pace not only lets your voice shine, but also exudes authority and thoughtfulness – it's a win-win!

Next up, articulation and clarity are key. Pay attention to pronouncing your words distinctly, making sure they're projected and easy to understand. This practice adds to your overall presence and helps establish that all-important authority.

And hey, vocal register isn't just about words, y'know? Your non-verbal cues matter too! Things like posture, body language, and facial expressions should align with the authority and presence you're aiming for. Stand tall, keep an open and confident posture, and let your lower-pitched voice do its thing.

Mastering the power of vocal register is an invaluable skill that can seriously up your communication game. So, take charge of that chest voice, my friend. Let it show off your authority, power, and presence in every interaction. Remember to practice regularly, use intentional pacing, articulate like a champ, and rock those confident non-verbal cues. Embrace the full potential of your lower register, and watch as your voice commands attention and leaves

Timbre

When it comes to effective communication, we all know words pack a punch. But, hey, let's not forget the impact of voice quality on how folks perceive our message. The texture and tone of our voice, aka timbre, play a crucial role in building connections and grabbing attention. In this section, we'll dig into why voice quality matters, explore ways to cultivate a smooth, rich, and downright enchanting voice, and unveil how tongue twisters jazz up articulation and timbre.

➡ The Power of Voice Quality

How we sound has a massive impact on how others see us and soak in what we say. A captivating voice quality can stir emotions, create engagement, and build trust. Research says people with a pleasing and resonant voice come across as more confident, trustworthy, and persuasive. So, let's invest some time in nurturing our voice quality to supercharge our communication skills.

➡ Craft a Velvety, Lush, and Cozy Voice

Mastering Breath and Diaphragmatic Control

Take deep breaths to strengthen that diaphragm and build some serious breath support. Stay mindful of your breath flow to maintain smooth, controlled speech. Hone your breath control game to project your voice with gusto and create some epic resonance.

Play with Resonance

Dabble in different vocal zones—your chest, nasal passages, even that noggin of yours. Vocalize specific sounds or vowels to get that sweet resonance where you want it, adding depth and richness. Let out some "hmm" or "mmm" sounds to create vibrations in your mouth and throat, giving you that warm, soulful voice.

Sharpen Articulation and Diction

Dive into those twisted tongue teasers to master articulation, clarity, and overall diction. Focus on crisp and precise pronunciation to deliver your words like a pro. Challenge yourself with tongue twisters at various speeds to level up your articulation skills and get your timbre flexing.

Tongue Twisters for Articulation and Timbre Magic

Tongue twisters ain't just silly word games; they're power tools for boosting articulation and cranking up the timbre. By diving into tongue twisters on the regular, you can:

Fine-Tune Articulation: These tongue twisters give your tongue, lips, and vocal muscles a workout, honing their teamwork and coordination. Your speech gets clearer, sharper, and more distinctive, making you sound like a polished pro.

Unlock Timbre Flexibility: Tongue twisters push your vocal abilities to the limit, making you dance through a range of sounds and textures. By conquering these challenging phrases, you gain masterful control over timbre's subtle nuances, allowing you to evoke various emotions and captivate any audience.

Boost Confidence: mastering tongue twisters builds your voice confidence. As you conquer intricate and rapid word patterns, you become at ease with the twists and turns of language, and your voice flows effortlessly, leaving your listeners spellbound.

Nurturing a smooth, velvety, and inviting voice is the key to forging connections and engaging your listeners. By understanding the power of voice quality, and by incorporating techniques like breath control, resonance exercises, and tongue twisters, you'll level up your articulation, timbre, and overall vocal delivery. Embrace the journey of unleashing your voice's potential, and watch as your captivating timbre transforms your communication, making a lasting impact on everyone you interact with.

Prosody

When it comes to communication, words ain't the only thing that matters. It's the whole shebang—the way we talk, the way we move—that helps us get our message across. And one big player in this game is prosody—the tune, rhythm, and tone of our speech. Prosody adds flavor and depth to our words, letting us express emotions, stress the important bits, and really connect with our audience. So, let's dive into the world of prosody, the power of changing our pitch for emphasis, and an exercise to pump up our prosodic skills.

➡ Prosody Packs a Punch in Communication

Prosody is like the secret sauce that gives our words that extra kick. It's all about pitch, stress, rhythm, and tone—how we say things, not just what we say. And these elements help us convey meaning and emotions, loud and clear.

One mighty role of prosody is to express emotions. Picture this: saying "I'm thrilled!" with a rising tone, letting that genuine excitement burst out, versus saying it flatly, without that same oomph. Prosody helps us hit 'em right in the feels, forging a deep connection and making our communication truly captivating.

But that's not all! Prosody also helps us put the spotlight on what really matters. By tweaking our pitch, stress, or rhythm, we can make certain words or phrases stand out like diamonds in the rough. It's like a secret weapon, helping us emphasize key points and guide our listeners through the maze of our message. With prosody, we can make even the trickiest of situations crystal clear.

➡ Pitch It Up, Stress It Out, and Roll with It

Now, let's turn up the volume on the power of pitch, that rising and falling rollercoaster that adds some spice to our words. By playing with our pitch, we can throw a spotlight on what's important, making those words pop like fireworks on the Fourth of July. Here are a few nifty tricks to nail that emphasis:

Rise and Shine: When you're asking a question or seeking confirmation, end with a pitch that's a little higher, like saying "You're coming to the party, right?" The rising intonation on "right" gives it that extra zing, making sure you get that thumbs-up.

Let It Fall: To bring on the certainty and finality, end your sentence with a lower pitch. Take a line like "I am confident we can achieve our goals" and let that pitch drop on "goals." Bam! You've just served up a dish of determination and assurance.

Stressed for Success: Give certain words a high-five by stressing them in your sentence. This creates contrast and turns up the spotlight. So, let's say "I never said you stole my wallet." By stressing different words like "never," "said," "you," "stole," "my," or "wallet," you can change up the whole shebang and get your point across loud and clear.

➡ Flex Those Prosodic Muscles with an Emotional Elevation Workout

Now, it's time to pump up your prosodic muscles and get flexin'! Here's an exercise that'll turn you into a prosodic superstar:

Pick a juicy passage, something short and sweet, from your favorite book, poem, or speech. Choose something that stirs up different emotions and lets you play around with the tune.

Read it out loud, my friend, and focus on the prosodic elements—the pitch, stress, rhythm, and tone. Get experimental! Try different ways of delivering those lines, tweaking the melody and rhythm to hit those emotional buttons. Let it flow, let it groove, and let your prosody shine!

So, there you have it, folks—the power of prosody, the rhythm and melody that can take your communication to a whole new level. Go forth and rock that prosodic magic!

Pace

Adjusting our speaking speed can help us highlight the juicy bits, captivate our audience, and keep 'em on the edge of their seats. So, let's dive into why adjusting our speed matters, the power of pace changes for impact, and an exercise to groove on those sentence rhythms and master pace variation.

➡ Importance of Adjusting Speaking Speed

Picture this: a Formula One race car zooming by at top speed, leaving you in the dust. How much of that epic scenery would you miss? Well, communication works the same way, my friend. When we talk at warp speed, our audience can get lost and miss the best parts. But if we crawl along like snails, we risk lulling 'em to sleep. That's why adjusting our speaking speed is crucial.

By mixing up our pace, we create a dynamic experience for our audience. Speeding up or slowing down intentionally can grab attention, build suspense, and hammer home the important stuff. It's like being a rockstar conductor, owning the tempo to stir up emotions and guide the crowd's understanding.

➡ Deliberate Changes in Pace for Impact

Just like a virtuoso musician who knows when to drop a sick beat or a smooth groove, a master communicator understands the impact of pace changes. Check out these tricks to harness the power of pace for maximum impact:

The Power Pause: Sometimes, silence screams louder than words. So, sprinkle intentional pauses at those juicy moments to let the good stuff sink in and amp up the anticipation. It's like hitting that pause button, lettin' the audience catch their breath and get ready for the next mind-blower. Pauses work like a charm before dishing out punchlines or shocking revelations, takin' the impact to a whole new level.

Rapid-Fire Delivery: When you wanna kick things into high gear, rev up that pace, baby! Speedin' up your speech brings the energy, pumps up the excitement, and screams urgency. This technique is perfect for spittin' out lists, facts, or stirrin' up that action-packed vibe. Just make sure you keep it clear and give your audience a chance to process the info.

Slow and Steady Wins the Attention: On the flip side, slowin' it down can be just as powerful. When you wanna make a point stick or build up the suspense, ease off the gas pedal. Droppin' your speed intentionally gives folks time to soak it all in, cranks up the anticipation, and says, "Something big's about to go down!" It's like stretchin' that rubber band before lettin' it snap, creatin' a jaw-dropping impact.

➡ Sentence Rhythms Exercise to Practice Pace Variation

To fine-tune your pace variation skills and become a true rockstar of sentence rhythms, try this exercise:

Pick a rockin' piece of text—could be from a book, an article, or a speech. Read that bad out loud and groove on the rhythm and flow of the sentences. Feel the natural cadence and pacing.

Now, switch it up! Experiment with different pacing techniques. Slow it down a tad for those key points or phrases, lettin' 'em sink in and make an impression. Then, rev it up for the sections that need energy and excitement. Find that sweet spot!

Pay close attention to the impact these changes in pace have on your delivery. Notice how mixin' it up keeps your audience engaged, highlights the good stuff, and keeps 'em beggin' for more.

So, get out there, own that stage, and ride that pace like a rockin' wave. With the right tempo, you'll have your audience eatin' outta your hand, beggin' for more.

Silence

In the grand jam session of communication, silence takes center stage, baby! Silence has the power to mesmerize, emphasize, and hit you right in the feels. In section, we're gonna dig deep into the importance of silence in effective communication, explore how strategic pauses bring reflection and emphasis to the party, and even throw in an exercise to help you master the art of silence like a pro.

➡ Role of Silence in Effective Communication

You know what they say: silence is golden! In the midst of the noise and chatter, silence creates a space where ideas can breathe, meaning can settle, and minds can truly connect. It's like hitting the pause button on a wild conversation, giving your words room to echo, your message time to sink in, and your audience a chance to soak up every drop.

Silence also works its magic by building bridges of understanding. When we embrace those quiet moments, we invite others to open up and share their thoughts and emotions. It's like giving them a VIP pass to the stage of communication, where their voices can shine. By honoring silence, we show respect, empathy, and create the perfect groove for genuine connection.

➤ Strategic Use of Pauses for Reflection and Emphasis

Just like a maestro knows how to work the crowd, a master communicator knows when to drop the beat and let the silence speak volumes. Strategic pauses add flavor, depth, and rhythm to your message, my friend.

When you rock a well-timed pause, you give your audience a chance to reflect. It's like pressing the "pause for thought" button and letting the magic unfold. These precious moments allow your listeners to process, ponder, and truly engage with what you're saying. It's all about creating a dialogue, a back-and-forth that makes the conversation groove and the ideas flow.

Pauses are also like spotlight moments, puttin' the spotlight on the juicy bits. By strategically sprinkling pauses before or after a killer statement, you draw attention to it like a moth to a flame. It's all about the emphasis. The pause adds weight, oomph, and makes those words hit home like a thunderbolt. It's like the dramatic pause before the punchline, setting the stage for the ultimate impact.

➤ Pausing Awareness Exercise for Mastering Silence

Now, let's crank up the volume and dive into a pausing awareness exercise that'll take your silence skills to a whole new level:

Find yourself a cozy spot where you can vibe without distractions. Peace and quiet!

Take a deep breath, center yourself, and get in the zone. It's all about the here and now.

Grab a snappy passage, a killer quote, or unleash your own writing prowess.

Read that bad boy out loud, payin' close attention to where natural pauses pop up. Feel the rhythm, the flow, and let the words carry you.

Now, let's crank up the funk! Read it again, but this time, throw in those deliberate pauses. Experiment with the length and placement of the pauses, like a DJ mixin' up the beats. Feel how the pauses change the whole vibe, emphasize certain words, and make your message shine.

Take a moment to reflect. Think about how silence can amp up your communication game, deepen connections, and make you a rockstar of understanding. Remember those moments when the pauses hit the sweet spot and groove with them in your everyday conversations.

'Cause here's the deal: silence ain't empty, it's full of potential. Embrace it, harness its power, and let it take your communication to heights you never knew existed.

As the legendary playwright Samuel Beckett once said, "Words are all we have; silence is all we need." So, embrace the silence, my friend, and let it be your secret weapon on the stage of communication.

Pitch

By tweakin' and twirlin' our pitch like a pro, we can unleash a whirlwind of emotions and meanings, takin' our message to a whole new level. We're gonna dive deep into the importance of pitch for emotional expression, explore the pitch ranges that lie within different emotions, and even toss in an exercise to help you master pitch control and unleash the true power of your expressive voice.

➡ Altering Pitch for a Wild Ride of Emotions

Picture this: a a singer belting out a heart-wrenching ballad or a comedian nailing that punchline like a boss. What makes their performance soar? It's all in the pitch! By mixin' it up, we tap into the realm of emotions and let 'em run wild. We can turn up the heat with a high-pitched frenzy, radiating enthusiasm, energy, and even a dash of tension. It's like cranking up the volume on our emotions, makin' 'em impossible to ignore. On the flip side, we can bring it down low, with a deep, resonant pitch that adds a touch of seriousness, mystery, or even a sprinkle of sadness. It's like laying down a deep bassline that vibrates through your soul.

When we embrace the magic of pitch variation, our words become an emotional masterpiece. We can splash 'em with colors, layer 'em with depth, and create a symphony of understanding. Pitch becomes our secret weapon, connecting us on a level that mere words can't touch.

➡ Exploring the Thrills and Chills of Pitch Ranges

Just like an artist mixin' hues on a canvas, we communicators dive into a wild range of pitches within each emotion. 'Cause emotions, they ain't one-dimensional. Oh no, they're complex creatures, full of shades, layers, and surprises. So, let's take joy, for instance. It can burst forth with a high-pitched laughter, joyous and infectious like a chorus of happy birds. Or it can sway with a melodic, upbeat tone, like a catchy tune you just can't resist. And sadness? Well, that can creep in with a low, melancholic pitch that tugs at the heartstrings. Or it can whisper through a soft, mournful sigh, like a gentle breeze on a rainy day.

Each emotion has its own pitch playground, and by takin' a wild ride through these ranges, we bring our communication to life. By explorin' the subtle variations within emotions, we become masters of emotional expression, strikin' chords that resonate with our listeners.

➡ Pitch Range Exercise

Now, let's get on board the emotion rollercoaster and tackle an exercise that'll make you the boss of pitch control and expand your emotional range.

Find yourself a cozy spot where you can let loose and explore your voice, no interruptions allowed. Get ready to unleash the beast within!

Pick a set of emotions that tickle your fancy. Joy, anger, surprise—whatever floats your boat.

Start by expressin' each emotion with your natural pitch range. Pay attention to how your voice naturally responds, and groove with the patterns that emerge. Let your emotions guide the way.

Now, let's push the limit! Experiment with different pitches within each emotion. Crank up the excitement with a sky-high pitch, or take it down low for a touch of solemnity. Play around with the whole spectrum in between. Feel the emotional rollercoaster take off as you explore every twist and turn of your voice.

Take note of how the intensity of each emotion changes, how different pitches impact the overall delivery, and the connection you feel with each ride.

Practice, practice, practice! Let yourself get comfortable and in tune with the full range of pitches available. Ride that emotion rollercoaster like a pro, and let your voice become the wildest ride of 'em all.

'Cause here's the deal: when you ride the emotion rollercoaster with pitch control, you become the conductor of a symphony that touches hearts and moves souls. So, buckle up and enjoy the ride!

Volume

By mixin' Volume up like a pro, we can add some serious dynamics, intensity, and a whole lotta punch to our message. We're gonna dig deep into why volume modulation is key to kickass communication, discover how it creates intimacy and grabs attention, and we ain't stoppin' there—we'll even throw in a rockin' exercise to help you master volume control and take your voice to stratospheric heights.

➡ Volume Modulation: Turnin' Up the Impact

Picture this: you're in a rowdy room, tryin' to get someone's attention. How do ya do it? You raise your voice, right? Pump up that volume and cut through the chaos like a boss. That's the power of volume modulation.

When we crank it up, we infuse our words with passion, energy, and a sense of urgency. It's like turning up the volume knob at a wild party—you create a buzz that'll have folks hangin' on your every word. But hold your horses, 'cause sometimes, lowering the volume can work its own magic. It draws people in, creatin' an air of intimacy and mystery. It's like whisperin' a secret that only the chosen few get to hear.

By gettin' a handle on volume modulation, we become the conductors of our communication symphony, knowin' just when to crank it up to eleven and when to bring it down to a seductive murmur. We'll snatch the attention of our listeners and have 'em beggin' for more.

➡ Intimacy and Attention: The Volume Combo

Volume ain't just about makin' a ruckus—it's about creatin' an experience. When we play with our voice volume, we create a sense of closeness that pulls people in. It's like havin' a heart-to-heart in a crowded room, where all the distractions fade away, and it's just you and the person listenin'.

Imagine this: someone leans in, lowerin' their volume, and whispers sweet nothings. It's magnetic, my friend. It makes you lean in too, eager to catch every word, like you're sharin' a juicy secret. On the flip side, when someone cranks up the volume, it's like a lightning bolt strikin'—it grabs attention and commands the room. It's a rallyin' cry that sets your soul ablaze.

Volume gives us the power to connect on a deep level. By skillfully mixin' up the volume, we create moments of intimacy, ignite emotions, and leave a lasting imprint on those who listen.

➡ Rockin' Exercise: Volume Control Unleashed

Now, let's dive into a kickass exercise that'll help you master volume control and take your communication skills to the next level:

1. Pick a passage from your favorite book, poem, or speech. Make sure it's got a rollercoaster of emotions and intensity levels.

2. Start by readin' the passage at a moderate volume, capturin' the overall vibe of the piece.

3. As you roll along, pinpoint the parts that need a volume boost to highlight the key points or convey some serious emotions. Crank it up and let your voice soar!

4. Next, spot the sections that call for a softer, more intimate touch. Dial it down, creatin' an atmosphere of closeness and intrigue.

5. Play around with different volume levels throughout the passage, findin' that sweet spot that captures the essence of each moment.

6. Record yourself while performin' the passage and give it a listen. Pay attention to the impact of volume modulation on the overall delivery and the emotions it stirs up inside ya.

7. Keep practicin' that passage, honin' your volume control skills, and gettin' comfy with the dynamic nature of communication.

By rockin' this exercise on the reg, you'll master volume modulation like a champ. You'll command attention, create intimacy, and leave folks speechless (in the best way possible). So, crank up that volume, and let your voice roar!

Section 2: Body Language

Body language it's a game-changer! Underestimate it and you're pushing your audience away. But nail it, and you'll have 'em eating out of your hand. So, what the heck is body language anyway? It's your body's way of talking without uttering a word. It's the combo of facial expressions, gestures, and movements that spill the beans on what's going on in your head. Picture this: how are you sitting or standing right now? What's that expression on your face? Smiling or frowning? Are you slouching or owning your space?

Imagine someone snapping a photo of you right now. What kind of vibes do you think people will get based on your body language? Will they think you're friendly and approachable or someone not to be messed with? Here's the kicker: body language often flies under the radar, meaning you can say one thing but your body screams the opposite.

Ever wondered why body language matters in communication? Well, let me spell it out for you: people can try to sound confident, but their body language spills the truth. They might say, "I'm thrilled to be here," but their face and gestures say otherwise. It's like meeting new folks and telling them you're stoked to meet them, but your body language shouts the opposite. You might think you rocked that social interaction, but truth is, those peeps probably weren't impressed. Something about your body language just didn't jive with them.

The thing is, our body language spills the beans about our inner emotions, even if we deny 'em or keep 'em locked away. It's like our bodies have a big mouth that can't keep secrets. So, when it comes to communication, body language can make or break you. Get it right, and you'll crush it. Let it get the best of you, and you're toast.

When you're prepping your speech, don't forget to work on your body language game too. Now, remember, body language works two ways: there's your body language (that's you) and your audience's body language.

The tips I'm about to drop will help both you and your audience. You'll learn not only how to rock the stage but also how to read your audience like a pro. Trust me, that skill will come in handy. You don't wanna be that presenter who thinks they're killin' it while boring their audience to death, do ya?

Now, let's dig into the nitty-gritty of body language. There are different types you gotta keep in mind. Brace yourself for a wild ride:

Eye contact. Yeah, even on stage, you gotta lock eyes with your peeps. You don't have to eyeball every single soul, but scan the crowd and connect with someone, anyone! If they're brave enough to meet your gaze, hold it for a sec or two. No need for a creepy stare-down, though. That'll freak 'em out. Eye contact helps you gauge their reaction. Interested or about to doze off? Yawning when someone's staring at you is a no-no, so they'll hide it. Eye contact also shows you're confident in your spiel.

Facial expressions. Don't be a poker face, my friend. Let your face shine like a beacon of emotions. Smile, smirk, raise an eyebrow, or give 'em the stink eye if needed. Your face is like a movie screen, and emotions are playing out on it. If your words are saying "exciting," but your face screams "boredom," guess what? Your audience will be confused or downright turned off. So, wear your emotions on your face like a fancy hat.

Gestures and movements. Here's where you gotta unleash your inner actor or actress. You're on stage, baby! Use your hands, your arms, your whole body if needed. But hey, don't be a flailing octopus. Make purposeful gestures that sync with your words. Are you talking about something big? Spread your arms wide like you're embracing the world. Going deep into a topic? Lean forward and captivate your peeps. Use your body like a storytelling tool. And if you're nervous, keep those fidgety hands under control. We don't want 'em running wild.

Posture and stance. Picture this: you're standing there, shoulders slouched, like you just don't care. How's that gonna look to your audience? Not so hot, my friend. Stand tall, like you're the king or queen of the stage. Hold your head high and own your space. And no, we're not talking about being stiff like a robot. Stay loose, but with confidence. If you're all hunched up, you'll look like you're about to bail. Let your body scream, 'I'm here, and I'm gonna rock your world!'

So, now you know the drill. Body language ain't no joke. It's the secret sauce that can make you a captivating speaker or a forgettable one. Pay attention to how you present yourself, and don't forget to read your audience too.

Section 3: The Importance of Creating Credibility & Trust

Let's dive into the crucial role of speaker credibility when it comes to effective communication. It's all about earning that trust and making your audience see you as a rock-solid communicator before they'll even consider buying into your arguments. Speaker credibility boils down to two key factors: competence and character.

➡ Grasping Competence

To establish your credibility as a speaker, you've got to flaunt your intelligence, knowledge, and expertise on the subject at hand. There are a few nifty ways to pull this off:

First things first, make it crystal clear why you're the authority on the topic. Share your educational background, professional experience, or any fancy certifications or achievements that back up your expertise. By laying out your credentials upfront, you'll give your audience a serious confidence boost. You can also draw on your personal experiences related to the topic, if you've got any. Share juicy anecdotes or real-life examples that offer up valuable insights and crank your credibility up a notch. It shows that you've got a good grip on the subject matter and you've walked the talk.

Lastly, don't forget to showcase the research you've done. Prove that you've dived deep into the topic, sifted through reputable sources, and come out the other side with a solid understanding. Sprinkle in some credible research, relevant stats, or studies to fortify your authority and establish yourself as a knowledge guru.

➡ Gaining Trust and Showing You Care

But hey, it's not just about being competent. Your character plays a big role in winning over your audience too. They need to see you as genuine, trustworthy, and genuinely concerned about their well-being. Here are a couple of neat tricks to emphasize your character:

- Find some common ground with your audience. Tap into their values, experiences, and concerns. Show that you get where they're coming from and acknowledge their perspectives. This connection helps build trust and creates a bon

- Highlight how your proposition aligns with their values and beliefs. When your audience sees that your arguments jive with their worldview, they're more likely to view you as someone they can count on. Show them how your proposed solution benefits them personally, professionally, or lines up with their moral compass.

Building Competence

It's all about flexing your knowledge and expertise. Check out these strategies to solidify your street cred when it comes to the subject matter.

Proving Your Qualifications: Sharing Relevant Experience

To boost your credibility, spill the beans on your relevant experiences that scream expertise. Talk about your hands-on involvement in the subject matter or any mind-blowing accomplishments that establish you as a force to be reckoned with.

For example, if you're speaking about marketing strategies, spill the beans on the killer campaigns you've spearheaded or the groundbreaking achievements you've unlocked in the field. By dishing out these experiences, you serve up tangible evidence of your expertise and cement yourself as a credible source.

Flaunting Your Research Skills: Establishing Your Authority

To drive home your competence, flaunt the research you've conducted on the topic. Explain how you've dug deep into trustworthy sources like scholarly articles, industry reports, or expert opinions. This shows that you've put in the legwork to really understand the subject matter.

Throw in specific studies or kick-ass statistics that back up your arguments. Weave in data-driven evidence to supercharge your claims. By doing this, you position yourself as an informed and credible speaker who relies on legit information.

Enhancing Character

Let's talk about character and why it's crucial for speaker credibility.

➡ Finding Common Ground: Getting on Their Wavelength

To build trust, you've gotta find some common ground with your audience. Dig deep and uncover shared experiences, values, or concerns that strike a chord. Emphasize these points of connection to create a sense of rapport and show that you really get where they're coming from.

For instance, if you're speaking about environmental conservation, shine a spotlight on the shared goal of preserving nature for future generations. Show them that, just like them, you're all about protecting the environment, and that your proposed actions align with their values.

➡ Matching Values and Beliefs

If you want to earn trust, your arguments need to align with your audience's values and beliefs. Get a good grasp on their core principles and frame your arguments accordingly.

Highlight how your proposition syncs up with their values. Point out the benefits they stand to gain or how your ideas fit right in with their existing beliefs. By doing this, you show that you understand and respect where they're coming from, fostering trust along the way.

Delivering with Flair: Confidence, Expression, and Smooth Talk

Alright, let's delve into the art of delivery and how it amps up your speaker credibility. This section is all about nailing your delivery and exuding confidence like a pro.

➡ Talking the Talk: Clear, Smooth, and on Point

To be seen as credible, you've gotta speak with fluency and clarity. Practice enunciating your words and keeping a steady pace. Steer clear of filler words and awkward pauses that can put a dent in your credibility. Use the learning of the previous sections.

Project that voice of yours, make sure everyone in the room can hear you loud and clear. Use the right intonation and emphasis to drive your message home. A fluent and articulate delivery notches up your credibility and helps your audience grasp your ideas without a hitch.

Embracing Emotion: Captivating the Crowd

A credible speaker knows how to express emotions that hit home with the audience. Emotion adds depth and authenticity to your message, making it all the more compelling. Vary your tone and wear your emotions on your sleeve. Let your facial expressions do the talking too. Share those personal anecdotes or examples that tug at the heartstrings and make your arguments relatable.

➡ Rocking the Confidence: Authenticity and Passion

Confidence is key. When you ooze confidence, your audience can't help but trust you and see you as the real deal. Here's how to get that confidence boost:

- Prepare like there's no tomorrow. Rehearse that speech of yours, get familiar with the content, and polish it till it shines. Practice in front of a mirror or even record yourself to catch any areas for improvement.

- Hold yourself with pride. Stand tall, make eye contact, and use gestures that scream confidence and conviction. Remember, your body language speaks volumes about your credibility.
- Let that passion of yours shine through. When you genuinely care about the topic, it radiates in your delivery. Infuse your speech with energy, speak from the heart, and let that passion captivate your audience. You'll establish yourself as an expert worth listening to.

Crafting Knockout Arguments: The Power of Persuasion

We're diving into the real meat of it: crafting arguments that pack a punch and make you one persuasive speaker. This section is all about constructing compelling arguments that leave a lasting impact.

➡ Structuring for Success: Intros, Body Slams, and Killer Conclusions

A well-structured speech is the name of the game. Make sure you've got a clear introduction, a solid body, and a killer conclusion. Recall the learnings from the part on crafting the message.

In that intro, give 'em a sneak peek of what's coming, establish your credibility, and lay down your main proposition. The body of your speech should dish out your arguments in a logical order, backed up by evidence and examples. And don't forget that conclusion! Summarize your key points, reinforce the importance of your proposition, and leave 'em with a lasting impression.

➡ Bringing in the Big Guns: Trustworthy and Relevant Evidence

To strengthen your arguments, you need some serious firepower. That means bringing in trustworthy and relevant evidence. Cite those credible sources like research studies, expert opinions, or top-notch publications. It shows that your claims are rooted in solid information.

Choose evidence that directly supports your main points and appeals to your audience's logic and reason. Statistics, case studies, and real-life examples are your secret weapons to supercharge your arguments and make 'em more persuasive than ever.

➡ Tackling Oppositions

Now, let's talk about tackling those counterarguments head-on. Acknowledging and addressing opposing viewpoints boosts your credibility like nothing else. Show 'em you're ready to take on the challenge. Anticipate those objections and bring your A-game to refute 'em. Prove that you've considered alternative perspectives and come prepared with strong counterarguments. This demonstrates your expertise and leaves no room for doubt or skepticism.

Conclusion

By nailing your competence and character, delivering with confidence, and crafting knockout arguments, you'll be a trusted and influential speaker in no time. Remember, building credibility takes time and practice, but with these strategies in your arsenal, you'll be unstoppable. So go out there, inspire change, and make your mark as a speaker worth listening to!

Section 4: Create an Emotional Connection

Let's dive into the juicy topic of building deep emotional connections, 'cause this world is seriously craving it. We've got way too many people shouting "me, me, me" and not enough folks who know how to connect with others. This leaves a whole bunch of folks starved for some genuine human connection. But guess what? It's your golden opportunity! If you learn the art of bonding and connecting, you'll be living the social life of a freaking king or queen. Trust me, everyone will be clamoring to hang out with you, men and women alike. Let me give you a step-by-step guide on how to make it happen:

Start with vibing: Instead of diving straight into the deep end, start by vibing with people. Think of it as having lively conversations that cover a wide range of topics. Keep it light-hearted, but don't shy away from going deeper when the moment feels right. You want that mix of breadth and depth, sprinkled with snippets of personal info. Just be careful not to get too deep too quickly.

Create comfort for opening up: The key here is to make people feel at ease enough to open up. It's all about your character and the way you handle things. Accept the dark side of people, including your own. Show genuine curiosity about others, 'cause that's how you'll learn more about them and life in general. Find joy in making people feel accepted and cherished, which naturally makes you accepting of them. And most importantly, embrace the pleasure of bonding and connecting. It's a two-way street, my friend!

Techniques for deepening the connection: Now let's get into some nitty-gritty techniques. Ask personal questions, but not in a creepy, interrogative way. Make it feel natural, like it's just a normal part of getting to know someone. Don't be afraid to ask deeper questions that explore their thoughts and feelings. Actively listen without passing judgment, show that you truly get them by empathizing, and share your own stories and experiences. This back-and-forth sharing is the real deal, my friend, creating that win-win connection. Just remember to keep the conversation light and positive when it starts feeling heavy.

Communicate trust and confidentiality: For deep sharing to happen, people need to trust you and believe that you'll keep their secrets safe. Be explicit about it, let them know that what they share with you stays with you. Stay cool and nonchalant, 'cause being too eager can make you seem untrustworthy. Give them space to express themselves, both verbally and nonverbally. Sometimes, silence can speak volumes. Think of yourself as a priest in the confession booth, my friend.

Find the right balance: It's important to strike a balance between depth and light-heartedness. Sure, going deep is great, but don't stay there forever. It can start feeling invasive or too serious. Remember, people want to have fun! So mix it up, my friend. Keep the conversation lively and sprinkle in those deep moments. Make 'em laugh, 'cause laughter releases oxytocin and builds that connection. Find the humor that's unique to both of you, and don't shy away from politically incorrect jokes if you both vibe with it. Just be mindful and test the waters early on.

Let them speak, no fixing allowed: Men, listen up! We have this tendency to want to fix things, including people. But when someone opens up to you, resist that urge to jump in with solutions or facts. Just let them talk. Give 'em the space to express themselves without feeling judged or schooled. Acceptance is the name of the game, and you'll earn some serious brownie points for it.

Create your own "us bubble": This is where the magic happens. As the connection deepens, you'll start creating inside jokes, shared experiences, and unique humor that only the two of you understand. This creates an "us bubble" that's exclusive to your bond. It's like your own secret language, and it strengthens the emotional connection like nothing else. Keep nurturing and building that bubble, my friend. It's your special sauce.

Remember, don't force it. Let it grow naturally, 'cause the best connections are the ones that happen organically. So go out there, spread your wings, and connect with people on a whole new level.

Emotional Power in Communication

When it comes to your communication, you gotta dig deep and tap into those emotional reservoirs. It's all about hitting your audience right in the feels, even if you're dishing out analytical, financial, or technical content. In fact, if you find yourself talking about those things all the time, it's super crucial that you understand how emotions work their magic on your listeners.

Now, I've got five killer ways for you to create an "emotional encounter" between you and your audience. Stick to these rules, and you'll skyrocket your influence. Most speakers out there just regurgitate content, and trust me, that rarely hits an emotional sweet spot. So, here's how you can bring that emotional power into your speeches and presentations:

➡ Feel the Feels with an Emotional Message.

Let me tell you, when it comes to speaking, it ain't about you or your fancy content. It's all about your audience. So, before you start crafting your masterpiece, ask yourself if what you're putting together is gonna serve your purpose. Get this—your job is to change thoughts, feelings, and actions. Yup, we're diving into the deep end of emotions here. Figure out how to ride that emotional wavelength, connect with your peeps, and change their lives for the better. And trust me, this goes way beyond just delivering plain ol' content. It's a whole new level, my friend.

➡ Show Some Heart.

Content can't survive on its own. It's your job to breathe life into it, creating an electric connection between you and your audience. The good news is, you don't need to put on a show. Just be yourself, my friend. Speak from the heart about something you truly believe in. Here's the secret sauce: Focus on building a relationship with your audience and forget about how you're doing. Don't fret about your performance, just engage those listeners, and watch how they respond. It's pure magic, I tell ya!

➡ Speak the Language of Emotion.

If you wanna move people, you gotta speak their language. And I'm not talking about English or Spanish here—I'm talking about the language of emotion. Trust me, it's not that hard to make emotional connections when you share a common interest. But to make it happen, you gotta sprinkle some emotional words and connotations into your speech. Forget "like" and "should." We want "love" and "must." Check this out: "I like this development" vs. "I love this solution!" See the difference? Choose words that sing, not mumble. Go for lightning, not a lightning bug. As Mark Twain once said, "The difference between the right word and the almost right word is the difference between lightning and the lightning bug."

➡ Create an Emotional Rollercoaster.

Let's face it, conveying information is as boring as watching paint dry. Why settle for educating when you can inspire? Why settle for motivating when you can light a fire under their seats? Heck, why settle for influencing when you can change lives? That's the key—creating an emotional experience for your audience. Don't be satisfied with being a walking encyclopedia. You're here to tell stories, to give them something to remember. Memos, PowerPoint decks, and meeting minutes can handle the dry stuff. But you, you're the one who needs to bring the meaning, the humanity, and the excitement!

➡ Open the Floodgates of Emotion.

How to unleash the emotional floodgates in your talks. If you want your audience to get all hyped up and emotionally invested, you gotta show 'em the way. If you're just standing there, emotionless like a robot, why should they care? If you're all about conveying information without a hint of humanity, they'll probably check out and hit the snooze button. Now, I get it, you ain't perfect, and your presentation ain't gonna be flawless. But every time you step up there, you're giving your audience a gift—a real, live person, taking risks, and putting it all on the line. Your willingness to do that, my friend, that's what grabs their attention, builds your leadership, and adds a dash of charisma. It opens the door for them to connect with you, and for you to connect with them. Remember, emotions flow both ways!

Follow these five rules, and you'll be unleashing a tsunami of emotions in your speeches.

Section 5: The Power of First Impressions

You won't believe what I'm about to tell you. Brace yourself! People often size you up in a blink of an eye. Blink! Bam! They've already formed their initial judgment about you, and get this—it happens in just a measly tenth of a second. Can you imagine? Talk about lightning-fast impressions! So, when you're out there trying to make your mark, you better make it count. You've got less than a second to leave 'em awestruck instead of all "meh." Are you ready for the challenge?

➡ The Opening Act: Setting the Tone Like a Pro

The opening act sets the tone. If you stumble right out of the gate, it's like shooting yourself in the foot. Trust me, ain't nobody gonna stick around for the rest of the show if you flop from the get-go. So, let me give you the lowdown on how to nail that opening and captivate your audience.

➡ Flash Those Pearly Whites: The Power of a Winning Smile

First things first, flash 'em those pearly whites. I can't stress this enough. Smiling ain't just about lookin' friendly—it's a magical trick backed by science. It helps you shed that anxiety like a snake sheds its skin. It's like a secret weapon against those pre-presentation jitters. So, here's what you do. Go the extra mile and plaster a grin on your face for a solid 90 seconds before stepping into the spotlight. That's right, I said 90 seconds! It's your secret recipe for relaxation and comfort, a surefire way to slay those nerves. Remember, a genuine smile can work wonders.

➡ Bring on the Laughter: Humor as Your Ally

Humor is a total game-changer. It's like a magic wand that transforms the atmosphere in the room. Crackin' a joke or two at the beginning does wonders. It shows your audience that you don't take yourself too seriously, and it breaks the ice like a sledgehammer on a frozen pond. And the best part? Humor is a language that everyone speaks. It don't matter if your crowd is young or old, male or female, or hails from different corners of the globe. A well-placed quip can hook 'em and reel 'em in, filling the room with laughter and joy. Embrace your funny bone and sprinkle some humor into your communication. It'll make all the difference.

➡ Stories that Connect: Bridging the Gap

Alright, listen up, because I'm about to drop some truth bombs about the power of personal stories. They're like little windows into your soul. They humanize you and bridge the gap between you and your audience. It's not just a one-way street anymore; it's a conversation, a connection. But here's the kicker: your story's gotta be riveting, raw, and relatable. It needs to grab 'em by the heartstrings and yank 'em in, forging an unbreakable bond between you and your captive listeners. So, dig deep, my friend. Share a tale that resonates, that touches their core. Open up and let them see the real you. That's how you make an impact.

➡ The Opening Punch: Make It Unforgettable

Hold on tight, because we're about to dive into the most crucial part—your opening punch. I've seen so many presenters stumble right outta the gate, and let me tell ya, it ain't a pretty sight. It's like shooting yourself in the foot with a cannon. Ouch! It ain't just a stumble; it's a full-blown message to your audience that you ain't prepared. So, here's the deal. Make it crystal clear from the get-go. Hit 'em with a powerful opener that leaves 'em gasping for more. Knock their socks off, blow their minds, and have 'em begging for the more.

➡ Conclusion: First Impressions That Last

First impressions—they're a big deal. They form in a blink of an eye. Don't you dare risk losing your audience before you even start by taking the easy way out and neglecting that crucial first impression. Give it your all, my friend, and make 'em remember you for all the right reasons. Now go out there and conquer that stage like a rockstar!

Section 6: Say Goodbye to Fillers and Wow Your Audience!

Understanding Fillers

The Party Crashers of Your Speech Alright, let's get real. Fillers are like unwelcome guests at your speech party. They're those sneaky little words, sounds, and phrases that don't add any real value. We want our audience hanging on to every word, not distracted by useless fluff. So, let's boot these party crashers out and keep our focus razor-sharp!

Categories of Fillers: Noises, Words, and Phrases, Oh My! Time to break it down, my friend. Fillers come in three flavors: there are those *quirky sounds* we make when our brain takes a spontaneous vacation - think "um," "uh," and "ah." Then we've got the *words and hedge words* like "well," "like," and "basically" that sneakily sneak their way into our sentences. And let's not forget *the phrases* that sound important but don't really do much to enhance our message. We're talking about classics like "you know," "I mean," and "at the end of the day." It's time to show them the exit!

The Whys Behind Our Love Affair with Fillers Now, let's dig into why we cling to these fillers like they're our long-lost buddies. Brace yourself for some truth bombs:

- Searching for the perfect word, Sometimes, our brain goes on a wild goose chase for that one word that'll make our sentence sparkle. Fillers are like placeholders, saying, "Hold on, I'm thinking, I'll get there!"
- The complexity conundrum, when we dive into deep, abstract topics, fillers tend to pop up more often than popcorn at the movies. It's like our brain does a little tango trying to express those mind-blowing ideas. But fear not, we'll conquer this!
- Confidence blues, fillers sneak in when we're not 100% sure about what we're saying. They give us a little breathing room to gather our thoughts and respond like a boss. It's time to unleash our inner confidence beast!
- Signaling "keep on listening", in everyday chitchat, fillers can be handy to let others know we're not done talking. They act as a social cue, saying, "Hey, I've got more to say, so don't interrupt me, alright?" Let's keep the conversation flowing!

Strategies to Banish Fillers and Speak with Impact

Get in the filler-free zone: It's time to crank up your self-awareness volume. Tune in and catch those fillers in action. Here's what you can do:

a) Tech to the rescue: Grab an app like Ummo to record your speech and get a transcript highlighting your fillers. It's like having your own personal fillers coach, ready to whip you into shape.

b) Playback detective: Listen to your speeches, audio, or video recordings and create a fillers hit list. Get to know your patterns and take charge!

c) Enlist a buddy: Rope in a friend, colleague, or mentor to be your fillers watchdog. They can give you real-time feedback by raising a hand each time they spot a sneaky filler. Teamwork makes the dream work!

Embrace the power of pauses: Take a beat, let the moment simmer, and then unleash your words like a tsunami. Embrace the magic of intentional pauses to obliterate those fillers. Remember: Pause. Think. Speak.

Practice like a rockstar: No, we're not

Practicing your speech can do wonders for filler reduction. Know your material inside out, so the words flow effortlessly. The more familiar you are, the less you'll rely on fillers. Get ready to rock that stage!

Keep it simple and take your time: Let's keep things straightforward. Short and sweet sentences are your allies in this epic battle against fillers. Complexity is the enemy! And don't be afraid to slow down. Give yourself the gift of time to catch those fillers sneaking up on you. It's all about clear communication and connecting with your audience.

Section 7: The Power of Silence

We have already introduced the importance of silence. It's like a secret weapon, a hidden gem that can work wonders in during your communication and speeches. It's smart, versatile, and can save your bacon when things go south.

Picture this: silence lets you take a deep breath, fill your lungs with fresh air, and fire up those brain cells. It's like an actor or an opera singer, breathing deep down in the belly, using every ounce of oxygen efficiently. On the flip side, when you're nervous or gabbing away like a speed demon, you tend to take shallow breaths, huffing and puffing like you just ran a marathon. No bueno, amigo, 'cause that doesn't give you the oxygen boost you need.

And hey, when you're up there and suddenly draw a blank, silence comes to the rescue. Instead of blurting out, "Oops, my brain's on vacation," just hit that pause button, stay cool as a cucumber, flash a confident smile, and let your thoughts catch up. Silence buys you time, without making you sound like a scatterbrain.

But here's the real magic of silence—it gives your audience a chance to digest and soak in what you just said. Especially those golden nuggets, those key takeaways that make your words shine. It's like hitting them with a powerful truth bomb, and then, bam! You let the silence work its magic, amplifying the weight of your words.

Silence paints you as a composed and self-assured speaker. Even if your nerves are doing the jitterbug inside, if you can pull off a calm and collected silence, you'll look like a boss up there, exuding confidence and credibility. It's like that secret sauce for faking it till you make it, my friend.

And guess what? Silence can be your punctuation mark, your smooth segue between different points and sections of your speech. It's like a well-timed pause that adds rhythm and flow to your talk, guiding your audience through the twists and turns of your words.

Being comfortable with silence is a game-changer, a secret weapon that every speaker should have in their arsenal. And you know what? I've got some quotes from other folks who also know the power of silence. They say silence is pure gold, and I couldn't agree more.

Remember, silence isn't just an absence of sound; it's a strategic tool that can make your words soar, your presence shine, and your audience hanging onto your every word. So embrace the power of silence, and let it work its magic for you.

Section 8: Enthusiasm and Energy

When it comes to communication enthusiasm and energy are very important. Believe it or not, focusing on this one thing gives you the superpower to win over your audience.

An increase in enthusiasm and energy have taken countless average speakers and turned them into good ones, transformed good ones into great ones, and even elevated great speakers to world-class status.

Enthusiasm is a choice. You got that right! If you sprinkle a little excitement into your talk and strut your stuff with a spring in your step, people can't help but pay attention. Your audience will match your level of enthusiasm, no more, no less. So, if you wanna captivate 'em, ignite that sparkle of enthusiasm within you.

- Rule 1: Avoid speaking about something you ain't enthusiastic about.
- And Rule number two: if you ever break rule number one, fake it till you make it, baby!

There's no such thing as a snooze-worthy topic. It's all about the speaker, my friends. No matter what you're talking about, your audience won't be more pumped than you are.

Believe it or not, nervousness can actually be mistaken for enthusiasm. Ain't that a twist? When we're nervous, we cut to the chase, speed up our speech, and start movin' around like nobody's business. And guess what? The same happens when we're genuinely excited! It's like a happy coincidence, ain't it?

As a speakers your can use nervousness to your advantage. When we channel that pent-up energy and turn it into enthusiasm, guess what happens? Our audience gets energized too!

Alright, now let's dive into foolproof ways to inject enthusiasm and energy into any speech. Listen closely 'cause this is where the magic happens:

- First off, speed up your tempo every now and then.
- Next up, crank up that volume at the right time! Speak a tad louder than your usual self, and you'll grab their attention. If you're naturally on the quieter side, push yourself to project that voice.
- Now, get those feet moving and start gesturing like there's no tomorrow. We all know we use our hands when we're chattin' one-on-one, right?

Here's a key tip: the bigger the room, the grander your gestures should be. Small gestures scream timidity, while big, bold movements radiate confidence and competence. So, go big!

Last but not least, play with your tone and emphasis. When you stumble upon an important word or concept, deliver it with gusto. Highlight those gems! And when it's appropriate, tone it down a notch or pause for effect.

Remember this: act enthusiastic, and you'll be enthusiastic. If you implement any of these tricks in your speech, you'll be seen as an above-average speaker. Your enthusiasm as a speaker is what can set you apart. So crank up that energy level and watch the magic unfold!

Section 9: Preparation and practice tips

It may sound obvious to highlight the importance of preparation and practice, however having the right approach and following the right tips can make a huge difference. It's all about recognizing what you're great at and where you need to improve, practicing with purpose, and getting comfy in your speeches.

To start off, you gotta figure out your purpose. Whether you're pitching a business idea or sharing your research, practice is key to making sure your audience doesn't get stuck counting your "umms" but actually understands. So, let's make a practice plan that's manageable and takes away the stress while boosting the quality of your presentations.

Now, there are plenty of areas in communication and speeches to work on, but we gotta focus on the ones that will level up your talk the most. That's why it's highly recommended to record yourself in action. Grab a video of about 5-10 minutes, capturing both your moves and your voice. If possible, get a trusted friend or colleague to give you feedback. Once you have that video, it's time to dig in and answer some questions.

Before you hit play, think about how it felt. What did you do well? Any areas you wish you could've rocked even harder? Now, it's time to watch the video and take notes. Jot down things that catch your attention, both the good and the not-so-good. Anything that works well? Anything that distracts? Did your mind start wandering at any point?

Okay, now that you've watched the video, how do you feel? Did anything sound or look distracting? Did your perception change after watching it? Maybe you thought you were nailing something that didn't come across so smoothly, or vice versa. If your attention drifted, what was it about that part that lost you?

Now, let's break it down into two parts: verbal and nonverbal. For the nonverbal side, rewatch the video but mute the sound. Take note of your body language. How's your posture? Does it shift throughout the talk? Any movements that feel distracting? Are you making eye contact with the imaginary audience or spending too much time glued to the screen? Look for patterns or habits that pop up.

When it comes to the verbal aspect, close your eyes or turn away from the screen and just listen to the audio. Pay attention to your voice. Was it strong and clear? Did you vary the volume and pace effectively? Did you strategically use emphasis to highlight your main points? Anything that was hard to follow or distracting, like filler words or repeated phrases?

Alright, now that you know your habits, let's focus on three areas that you feel are most important to improve. Think about what will eliminate distractions and make your message shine. And here's the key: let's shift our focus from problems to solutions. Instead of obsessing over what not to do, let's find positive ways to make it better. For example, if filler words are a concern, try incorporating pauses whenever you catch yourself using them. Don't be afraid to step out of your comfort zone during practice. Sometimes, the seemingly extreme or uncomfortable things we try can lead to breakthroughs.

Now, we don't wanna overwhelm ourselves, so let's practice in manageable chunks. Our brains can only handle so much at once, right? So, let's work on one solution at a time, but repeat it a few times in a row. This gradual approach helps us improve with each round. Once you feel confident with one solution, move on to the next. After practicing each one individually, you can start combining them. It'll feel easier once you've honed in on each aspect. And to be ready for unexpected disruptions.

Create a practice plan that fits your schedule and stick to it. Break it down into shorter sessions that you can fit in between your other commitments. More frequent but shorter practices can do wonders, even if you're super busy. You can even think to practice talks in your head while walking home to work for example. Talk about efficient, right? So, visualize your speech, think about the verbal and nonverbal aspects, and own that content without even uttering a word.

Section 10: Small Talks Essentials

Ever wondered how some folks effortlessly waltz into a social gathering and start yapping away to anyone about anything, keeping the convo alive without a hitch? Well, what if I told ya that you could do the same? Buckle up, my friend, 'cause I'm about to spill the beans on how you can nail small talk like a pro. Let's face it, small talk ain't everyone's cup of tea, but when you've got it down pat, it's the bee's knees for connecting with people and creating a friendly vibe. It's like a warm-up before diving into the deep end of conversation, ya know?

But hey, if you ain't no social butterfly, I get how intimidating it can be. Believe me, I used to be as awkward as a penguin in the desert. It bugged me big time 'cause making new friends and connections felt like cracking a nut with a sledgehammer. So, I rolled up my sleeves, put in some elbow grease, and practiced like there was no tomorrow. And lemme tell ya, soon enough, I was chatting up folks left and right, smooth as silk, without breaking a sweat or making 'em uncomfortable. Now, let me share my tried-and-true tips to boost your small talk game. Brace yourself, 'cause we're diving right in.

Get Practicing Those Small Talks Everywhere

If you wanna level up, you gotta put in the work. You can't expect to be a small talk maestro if you only practice at fancy networking events or wild parties. That's like learning to ride a bike by watching a YouTube video. Nope, that ain't gonna cut it.

Small talk is all about kick-starting convos and keeping 'em flowing like a river. So here's the deal: set yourself a goal to initiate a certain number of small talks each day. Start with one, then ramp it up to ten. It might sound like a tall order, but believe me, you got this. Chat up your colleagues at work, shoot the breeze with shop assistants and cashiers, and reach out to long-lost friends. The more you push yourself, the faster you'll grow.

Forget About Trying to Be Interesting; Just Be Interested. Small talk ain't about hogging the spotlight and dazzling folks with your captivating tales. Nah, that's a surefire way to sink the conversation faster than a lead balloon. Picture this: you're at a party, and a stranger starts babbling about their life story. You'd be like, "Whoa, hold your horses, pal. I didn't sign up for a monologue!"

If you wanna rock the small talk arena, flip the script. Show genuine curiosity in the other person. Ask 'em the right questions, sit back, and listen like your life depends on it. Trust me, people love it when someone shows interest in what they have to say.

Master the Art of Asking the Right Questions

Now, listen closely 'cause this is the secret sauce. The best questions in small talk are the ones that tap into the here and now. We're talkin' situational questions that make sense in the moment. Take a gander around you and fire away with something that fits the scene. Like, "How do you know the host? Any juicy stories from your college days? What's the scoop on this shindig?"

You can also throw in a compliment about the person and then dig deeper. It's all about keeping it light, relatable, and natural.

Expand on or Diverge from the Small Talk

Alright, you've sparked a conversation. Now what? Well, think on your feet and keep the ball rollin'. When one topic leads to another, don't be shy to explore different avenues. Let's say you're at a birthday party in a lush garden, and you asked how the person knows the birthday celebrant. They spill the beans and mention they've been buddies since college. Boom! You got options, my friend.

Option 1: Dive deeper into their college days with follow-up questions like, "What were your majors? Any crazy stories or unforgettable moments? Did you have any classes together?"

Option 2: Take a detour from the small talk highway and switch gears to a related topic, like, "Speaking of college, have you been to any epic reunions or get-togethers? What are your favorite hobbies outside of work or school?"

Remember, keep the convo flowin' like a river, and actively listen to what they share. By showing genuine interest, you create a safe space for 'em to open up and keep the ball bouncin'.

Share Relatable Experiences or Anecdotes

When the moment is right, jump into the ring and share your own stories and experiences. This ain't a one-way street! By chiming in with your own tales, you build a bridge between you and the other person. Let's say the topic is college days, and they're sharing a wild adventure. Don't just sit there like a bump on a log! Jump in with your own story, like, "Man, I remember pulling an all-nighter for a project. Ever had any crazy deadline stories?"

Or maybe you're chattin' about hobbies, and they mention their love for hiking. You can add your two cents, sayin', "Funny you mention hiking. I recently started hittin' the trails, and it's been a mind-blowing way to connect with nature. Do you have any other outdoor activities you enjoy?"

Pay Attention to Non-Verbal Cues

Keep those peepers open! Non-verbal cues are the secret language of small talk. Watch out for body language, facial expressions, and tone of voice. They'll give you a sneak peek into the other person's interests and comfort level. If you spot signs of boredom or discomfort, it's time to gracefully wrap up the small talk and switch gears. Trust your gut and move on to greener pastures.

Practice Active Listening

Active listening is like having a superpower in the world of conversation. It means being fully present, giving 'em your undivided attention. Nod your head, lock eyes, and respond like you mean it. Show 'em you're hangin' on their every word. It ain't just about making 'em feel valued; it's about gatherin' intel to keep the convo sailin' smoothly.

Remember, practice makes perfect! The more you dive into small talk armed with these tips, the smoother and more confident you'll become. Don't sweat it if you stumble or feel awkward at first. It's all part of the learning curve. So get out there, embrace the art of small talk, and enjoy connecting with new folks. You got this, my friend!

Section 11: Basics of Persuasions Techniques

Have you ever wondered how successful individuals and famous businesses manage to win people over effortlessly? Well, it's all about the art of persuasion! These sneaky little tricks work their magic on our subconscious, delivering outstanding results when used correctly. So, buckle up and get ready to explore the eight most powerful persuasion techniques out there. Based on Robert Caldini's influential book, "Influence: Science & Practice."

The Foot in the Door Technique: Start Small, Win Big

Picture this: You want your friend to help you move, but asking them directly might be a bit too much. So, you start with a small favor like borrowing their truck for a quick errand. Once they're on board with that, it becomes much easier to ask for the bigger request—the actual move. It's like building a solid foundation before reaching for the stars!

The Door in the Face Technique: Aim High, Settle Smart

This one's a classic. Begin by asking for something grandiose or downright unreasonable, fully aware that it will be rejected. Then, when you follow up with a more reasonable request, it suddenly seems like a piece of cake! It's like asking your boss for a month-long vacation and settling for a long weekend instead. The key is in making the second request seem much more reasonable and achievable in comparison.

Anchoring Technique: Set the Bar, Influence the Outcome

When making decisions, we humans have a knack for comparing options. The Anchoring Technique takes advantage of this tendency by establishing an initial reference point or anchor. Imagine you're shopping for a new laptop, and you stumble upon a shiny model priced at $2,000. Suddenly, the other options seem more affordable in comparison, even if they're still quite pricey. The initial price acts as a mental anchor, influencing our perception of value.

Commitment & Consistency Technique: Small Steps, Big Influence

We all strive to be consistent in our actions and beliefs. Once you get someone to commit to a small favor, you can leverage that commitment to gain more significant support. It's like building a staircase, one step at a time. Start with something small, like asking your colleague to join you for a quick coffee break. Once they've committed, it becomes easier to ask for their assistance on a larger project. Consistency is the glue that holds relationships together!

Social Proof Technique: Join the Bandwagon, Embrace the Crowd

As social creatures, we often look to others for guidance when making decisions. The Social Proof Technique capitalizes on the power of the herd mentality. Imagine you're strolling through a new town, searching for a place to eat. If you stumble upon a packed restaurant with a line out the door, you're more likely to think, "Hey, this place must be good!" and join the hungry crowd. The actions of others influence our own choices, so hop on that bandwagon!

Authority Technique: Establish Credibility, Gain Trust

We naturally look up to those who possess authority or expertise in a specific field. The Authority Technique taps into this inclination by positioning yourself as an authority figure. It's like strutting your stuff in front of a captive audience, showing off your expertise and earning their trust. When companies proudly display their awards or highlight their appearances in major media outlets, they're leveraging the power of authority to win you over.

Scarcity Technique: Fear of Missing Out, Act Now!

The fear of missing out is a potent motivator. When something is scarce or limited, our desire for it intensifies. It's like trying to snag the last piece of a delicious cake before it disappears forever. Businesses use this technique by creating a sense of urgency and scarcity. Think of limited-time offers or products that are flying off the shelves. Suddenly, you feel compelled to act quickly before you lose out on a fantastic opportunity.

The Liking Technique: Friendship Wins Hearts

We tend to say "yes" more often to people we know, like, and trust. The Liking Technique revolves around building a genuine connection and finding common ground with the person you're trying to persuade. It's like discovering that you and your new neighbor are both die-hard soccer fans. Instantly, a bond forms, making it easier to convince them to join your weekend soccer league. When people like you, they're more likely to say "yes" to your requests.

These persuasion techniques have been studied and proven time and time again. From the famous "Foot in the Door" to the enticing power of scarcity, they tap into our subconscious and guide our decision-making. But remember, with great power comes great responsibility! So, use these techniques ethically and responsibly to create win-win situations.

Case Studies

Now, let's dive into a couple of fascinating case studies to see these techniques in action.

In 1966, researchers Jonathan Freedman and Scott Fraser conducted a study on the "Foot in the Door" technique. They divided women into groups and started by asking some simple questions about their kitchen products. Three days later, they followed up with a request to go through their kitchen cabinets and catalog their products. The groups that had initially answered the questions had a much higher compliance rate compared to the group that was only approached with the second request. This study showcased the power of the "Foot in the Door" technique.

Another intriguing case study revolves around the "Anchoring" technique. The Economist, in their subscription options, used an interesting pricing strategy. They presented three options: an online subscription for $59, a print subscription for $125, and a print & web subscription also for $125. Surprisingly, the majority of participants chose the print & web option. However, when the print option was removed, the preference shifted towards the online subscription. The presence of the print option acted as an anchor, making the print & web option appear more appealing. This case study demonstrates how anchoring can influence decision-making.

Cialdini and colleagues conducted an experiment with "The Door in the Face" technique where they first asked college students if they would volunteer to chaperone juvenile delinquents on a day trip to the zoo, which was met with widespread refusal. Then, they followed up with a more reasonable request of mentoring the delinquents for just two hours a week. The compliance rate increased significantly compared to a control group.

Commitment & Consistency Technique: A study conducted by Moriarty and colleagues focused on encouraging individuals to reduce energy consumption. Participants who made a public commitment to saving energy by signing a pledge were more likely to follow through with their commitment and implement energy-saving behaviors compared to those who did not make a public commitment.

| Part 5 | Highlights from some of the Best Speeches of All Times

Please note that the examples provided are intended for analysis purposes and do not advocate for any specific political view. If you wish to explore these speeches further, we encourage you to research them independently from reputable sources.

Martin Luther King Jr. - "I Have a Dream" speech (1963)

- Powerful repetition of the phrase "I have a dream" throughout the speech, emphasizing the vision of racial equality and justice.
- Utilization of vivid imagery and metaphors to paint a picture of a more harmonious and inclusive society.
- Addressing the crowd's emotions and aspirations, connecting with their shared experiences and hopes for a better future.
- Highlighting the urgency and the moral imperative for change, invoking a sense of justice and righteousness.
- Emphasizing the importance of nonviolent resistance and peaceful protest as a means to achieve social transformation.
- Appealing to the American values of freedom, equality, and justice, invoking the nation's founding principles and demanding their realization for all citizens.

Winston Churchill - "We Shall Fight on the Beaches" speech (1940) and "Their Finest Hour" speech (1940)

- Evoking a sense of national unity and determination during a time of crisis.
- Utilizing powerful rhetoric to inspire resilience and fortitude in the face of adversity.
- Acknowledging the challenges and sacrifices ahead while instilling hope and confidence in ultimate victory.
- Addressing the British people directly, fostering a sense of shared responsibility and purpose.
- Emphasizing the importance of staying steadfast and resolute in the fight against tyranny and oppression.
- Using vivid language and imagery to evoke a sense of courage, heroism, and national pride.

Mahatma Gandhi - "Quit India" speech (1942)

- Calling for mass civil disobedience and nonviolent resistance against British colonial rule.
- Appealing to the Indian people's sense of unity, self-reliance, and national identity.
- Advocating for peaceful protest as a means to dismantle oppressive systems and achieve independence.

- Highlighting the moral superiority of nonviolence, stressing its power to transform both the oppressor and the oppressed.
- Encouraging self-sacrifice and personal discipline as essential components of the freedom struggle.
- Inspiring hope for a future free from colonial rule, envisioning an inclusive and just society.

Abraham Lincoln - Gettysburg Address (1863)

- Opening with a powerful and memorable phrase, "Four score and seven years ago," setting the tone for the speech.
- Reflecting on the significance of the American Revolution and the principles of liberty and equality.
- Honoring the sacrifices made by the soldiers in the Civil War and framing their actions as a dedication to the cause of freedom.
- Emphasizing the unity and indivisibility of the nation, appealing for reconciliation and healing in a time of division.
- Reiterating the importance of preserving the democratic ideals of government of the people, by the people, and for the people.
- Expressing a commitment to the unfinished work of ensuring equality and justice for all citizens.

Nelson Mandela - "An Ideal for Which I am Prepared to Die" speech (1964):

- Demonstrating unwavering commitment and resilience in the face of oppression and injustice.
- Advocating for a democratic and inclusive society that transcends racial boundaries.
- Rejecting racial hatred and promoting forgiveness and reconciliation as essential components of nation-building.
- Calling for international solidarity and support in the struggle against apartheid.
- Appealing to the conscience of the oppressors and challenging them to recognize the humanity and dignity of all individuals.
- Inspiring hope and determination for a future South Africa free from racial discrimination.

Maya Angelou - Various speeches promoting social justice, equality, and women's rights:

- Utilizing poetic language and lyrical delivery to engage and captivate the audience.
- Sharing personal stories and experiences to create empathy and foster a connection with the audience.
- Advocating for the empowerment of marginalized communities and the importance of intersectionality.

- Inspiring resilience, self-love, and confidence in the face of adversity.
- Promoting unity and solidarity among diverse groups, emphasizing the strength in embracing our differences.
- Encouraging individuals to use their voices and take action to bring about positive change.

Ronald Reagan - "Tear Down this Wall" speech (1987)

- Issuing a bold challenge to Soviet leader Mikhail Gorbachev to dismantle the Berlin Wall and end the Cold War.
- Emphasizing the power of freedom and democracy in contrast to the oppressive nature of totalitarian regimes.
- Appealing to shared values and aspirations of the German people, seeking their support for reunification.
- Using strong and direct language to convey resolve and determination.
- Presenting the United States as a beacon of liberty and encouraging other nations to embrace freedom.
- Creating a moment of historical significance by positioning the speech at the symbolic Berlin Wall, highlighting the importance of the event.

Barack Obama - "A More Perfect Union" speech (2008):

- Addressing the complex issue of race in America with honesty and empathy.
- Sharing personal experiences and stories to foster understanding and bridge divides.
- Calling for unity and a common purpose beyond racial divisions.
- Expressing optimism and hope for a future of progress and inclusivity.
- Acknowledging the ongoing challenges of racial inequality while emphasizing the resilience of the American people.
- Emphasizing the importance of dialogue and listening to different perspectives in order to find common ground.

Elizabeth I - "Speech to the Troops at Tilbury" (1588)

- Rallying the troops and instilling courage and loyalty in the face of imminent war.
- Demonstrating strong leadership and commitment to defending the nation.
- Inspiring national pride and invoking a sense of duty and sacrifice.
- Using rhetorical devices, such as repetition and appeals to honor and glory, to motivate the troops.
- Conveying confidence in victory and assuring the troops of her unwavering support.
- Positioning herself as a symbol of strength and resilience, embodying the spirit of the nation.

Cicero - "First Oration Against Catiline" (63 BCE):

- Condemning Catiline's conspiratorial activities and rallying public support against him.
- Utilizing persuasive rhetoric and powerful language to sway public opinion.
- Presenting evidence and logical arguments to expose Catiline's intentions and discredit him.
- Calling for unity and cooperation among the Roman people to defend the Republic.
- Establishing himself as a defender of justice and the rule of law.
- Highlighting the dire consequences of inaction and the urgency of the situation.

William Shakespeare - Known for powerful monologues and speeches in his plays:

- Creating memorable characters with distinct voices and perspectives.
- Using poetic language and imagery to convey complex emotions and ideas.
- Exploring universal themes and timeless human experiences through his speeches.
- Addressing the audience directly, breaking the fourth wall and engaging them in the narrative.
- Balancing humor, wit, and pathos to evoke a range of emotions.
- Incorporating rhetorical devices, such as soliloquies and asides, to provide insight into characters' inner thoughts and motivations.

Susan B. Anthony - Known for speeches advocating for women's suffrage and equal rights

- Challenging societal norms and advocating for gender equality.
- Presenting logical arguments and evidence to support the cause of women's suffrage.
- Appealing to principles of justice, fairness, and democracy.
- Emphasizing the importance of women's voices and perspectives in shaping society.
- Inspiring women to stand up for their rights and participate in the fight for equality.
- Demonstrating courage and determination in the face of opposition.

John F. Kennedy - Inaugural Address (1961)

- Issuing a call to action and inspiring civic engagement.
- Emphasizing global responsibility and the importance of international cooperation.
- Encouraging citizens to be active participants in democracy.
- Utilizing rhetorical devices, such as antithesis and parallelism, to create memorable phrases and evoke emotion.
- Expressing a commitment to freedom, peace, and justice.
- Inspiring hope and confidence in a new era of progress and change.

Frederick Douglass - "What to the Slave is the Fourth of July?" speech (1852)

- Confronting the hypocrisy of celebrating freedom and independence while slavery still exists.
- Exposing the injustices and cruelty of the institution of slavery.
- Using powerful and vivid language to convey the experiences and struggles of enslaved individuals.
- Challenging the audience to confront their own complicity and take action against slavery.
- Advocating for the universal rights and dignity of all individuals, regardless of race.
- Demonstrating the power of storytelling and personal narratives to inspire empathy and social change.

Malala Yousafzai - United Nations Youth Assembly speech (2013):
- Sharing her personal experience as an advocate for girls' education and surviving an assassination attempt.
- Expressing resilience and determination in the face of adversity.
- Calling for global attention and action on girls' education and women's rights.
- Inspiring young people to stand up for their rights and believe in their power to create change.
- Emphasizing the transformative power of education in breaking cycles of poverty and discrimination.
- Appealing to universal values of equality, peace, and justice.

J.K. Rowling - Harvard Commencement speech (2008):
- Drawing upon personal experiences and setbacks to deliver a message of resilience and perseverance.
- Exploring the themes of failure, imagination, and empathy.
- Encouraging graduates to embrace their own unique journeys and not fear failure.
- Advocating for the power of imagination and storytelling to foster empathy and understanding.
- Highlighting the importance of using one's privilege and influence to make a positive impact on the world.
- Inspiring graduates to pursue meaningful work and contribute to the betterment of society.

Help Us!

Let us know how thrilled are you about having this book by leaving a quick review (it will take 1-2 minutes) by scanning the QR code below. The best way to do it?

- Upload a brief video with you talking about how you feel about the book.

- If that is too much, not a problem at all! A review with a couple of pictures of the book and/or just with a sentence or two (although the longer the better!) would be very helpful!

P.S. You do not have to feel obliged but for independent publishers reviews are the lifeblood. It will be very appreciated, deeply valued, and it helps a lot independent publishers like us.

Scan the QR-code below to leave a review

Get Your Bonus Content – What to Do

<u>Accessing the Bonus Content first will benefit you in going through this book</u>

To access scan the QR Code below:

Or go to the following link → rebrand.ly/ec-bonus1

Made in the USA
Las Vegas, NV
02 November 2023

79889594R00079